Also in the Children's Television Workshop Family
Living Series

Parents' Guide to Feeding Your Kids Right:
Birth Through Teen Years

Parents' Guide to

Raising Kids Who Love to Learn

Infant to Grade School

• • • • • • • • • • • • •

CHILDREN'S TELEVISION WORKSHOP

Preface by David Elkind

Prentice Hall Press

• • • • • • • • • • • • •

New York   London   Toronto   Sydney   Tokyo

CHILDREN'S TELEVISION WORKSHOP

Chairman—Chief Executive Officer: Joan Ganz Cooney
President: David Britt
Publisher: Nina Link

Series Editor: Marge Kennedy
Associate Editor: Sima Bernstein
Child Development Consultant: Istar Schwager, Ph.D.
Senior Writers: Russell Miller and Karyn Feiden

 Prentice Hall Press
Gulf + Western Building
One Gulf + Western Plaza
New York, New York 10023

Copyright © 1989 by Children's Television Workshop

Library of Congress Cataloging-in-Publication Data

Parents' guide to raising kids who love to learn : infant to grade
   school/Children's Television Workshop; preface by David Elkind.
   —1st ed.
     p.   cm.—(Children's Television Workshop family living
   series)
     Includes index.
ISBN 0-13-648833-1 (pbk.): $9.95
   1. Early childhood education. 2. Education, Preschool—Parent
participation. 3. Child development. I. Elkind, David, 1931-
II. Children's Television Workshop. III. Series.
LB1140.2.P357 1989
372'.21—dc19   88-38097
                                                             CIP

Designed by Laurence Alexander and Patricia Fabricant

Manufactured in the United States of America
10 9 8 7 6 5 4 3 2 1
First Edition

Acknowledg

• • • • • •

The editors wish to thank PJ Dempsey of Prentice Hall Press for the knowledge and assistance she offered in preparing and editing this series. We also wish to acknowledge the many contributions of David Elkind, Ph.D., our preface writer, and our advisory panel whose names and affiliations are listed on pages vii–ix; the writers of this volume, Russell Miller, Karen Feiden, and others listed on pages xi–xiii; and researchers Diane O'Connell, Jeanette Leardi, and Judith Rovenger.

Advisory Panel

......

HARRIET K. CUFFARO, Ed.D., is a member of the graduate faculty at Bank Street College of Education. In this role, Dr. Cuffaro teaches courses, supervises teachers, and directs an intern program. As a curriculum specialist, she has contributed to the development of nonsexist and multicultural programs and materials. Her publications reflect her interest in issues of equity and young children's dramatic play.

DAVID ELKIND, Ph.D., our preface writer, is Professor of Child Study and Senior Resident Scholar at the Lincoln Filene Center at Tufts University. Dr. Elkind has published well over three hundred works, ranging from journal articles on his research in human development to children's stories. He is also the author of twelve books, including his three most recent titles: *The Hurried Child, All Grown Up and No Place to Go,* and *Miseducation.* Professor Elkind just completed his term as President of the National Association for the Education of Young Children.

GERALD LESSER, Ph.D., is Bigelow Professor of Education and Developmental Psychology at Harvard University. Dr. Lesser's affiliation with the Children's Television Workshop began with the company's formation in 1968. Since that time, he has participated in the Workshop's decisions about the educational, research, and production goals of its television programs. Dr. Lesser currently serves as Chairman of the Board of Advisors of the Children's Television Workshop.

LUBERTA MAYS, Ed.D., is Dean of Academic Affairs at Medgar Evers College, CUNY. A former nursery school and Head Start director, her background also includes serving as a principle performer in an early childhood television series. Dr. Mays has been involved in developing early childhood programs in the Virgin Islands and West Africa. She holds an Ed.D. from Teachers College, Columbia University in Early Childhood Programs.

HANNAH NUBA, M.S., is Director of The New York Public Library Early Childhood Resource and Information Center. She holds a master's degree from Columbia University as well as certification in education and library science from the University of the State of New York. Her publications include *Resources for Early Childhood* and *Infants: Research and Resources.*

ISTAR SCHWAGER, Ph.D., is Director of Research for the Children's Television Workshop's Magazine Group—including the *Sesame Street Magazine Parents' Guide.* She has worked on the development of television shows, books, toys, and other products. She holds a doctorate in educational psychology and a master's degree in early childhood education. Dr. Schwager has taught at levels from preschool to graduate school and writes frequently for parents.

RONALD SPIEGEL, M.D., is a pediatric neurologist at Children's Hospital of St. Paul in St. Paul, Minnesota. Dr. Spiegel's medical training includes a residency in pediatrics at the University of Michigan Hospitals and a fellowship in pediatric neurology at the University of Iowa Hospitals. He is board certified in pediatrics and child neurology.

DOROTHY STRICKLAND, Ph.D., is Professor of Education in the Department of Curriculum and Teaching at Teachers College, Columbia University. Prior to working as a teacher educator, Dr. Strickland spent eleven years teaching in the New Jersey School system. Her publications include the books *Listen Children, Family Storybook Reading, Educating Black Children, Emerging Literacy: Young Children Learn to Read and Write,* as well as many journal articles. Professor Strickland is a past president of the International Reading Association.

DAVID WEIKART, Ph.D., is the President of High/Scope Educational Research Foundation. Through his work with High/Scope, Dr. Weikart has been involved in long-term studies of the effects of educational programs on the lives of children. Dr. Weikart holds a master's degree in Education and a Ph.D. in Education and Psychology from the University of Michigan.

BURTON WHITE, Ph.D., is the Director of the Center for Parent Education in Newton, Massachusetts. He has held many key positions in the field of education, including Senior Consultant, Missouri New Parents as Teachers; Principal Investigator, Brookline Early Education Project; and Director, Harvard Preschool Project. Dr. White is the author of *The First Three Years of Life* and holds a Ph.D. in Psychology from Brandeis University.

About the Writers

• • • • • •

KARYN FEIDEN is a New York City–based, freelance writer and editor with extensive credits in the fields of health and education. She is the author of *Sick and Tired: Coping with Chronic Fatigue Syndrome* (Prentice Hall Press), a contributor to *Parents' Guide to Children's Medications* (Bantam) and *The Job Sharing Handbook* (Ten Speed Press), and the editor of a health-care newsletter.

RUSSELL MILLER has taught students of all ages—from first graders in New York City to graduate students at Harvard. A former editor at *3-2-1 Contact*, the Children's Television Workshop's science magazine, he has twice won distinguished achievement awards from the Educational Press Association. He has written for the *Village Voice*, *Newsday*, and *Sesame Street Magazine Parents' Guide*, among others.

Credits

The following materials have been exerpted or adapted from the *Sesame Street Magazine Parents' Guide* or other Children's Television Workshop publications as noted. Copyright © Children's Television Workshop unless otherwise noted.

Chapter Four

Copple, Carol, Ph.D. "Learning Language." March 1988. Copyright © Carol Copple, Ph.D.

Kovacs, Deborah. "Wordplay." March 1988.

Schwager, Istar, Ph.D. "Getting Ready to Read." October 1985.

Chapter Five

Schwager, Istar, Ph.D. "Math Is More Than Numbers." November 1986.

Chapter Six

Copple, Carol, Ph.D. "Games Children Play." March 1987. Copyright © Carol Copple, Ph. D.

Copple, Carol, Ph.D. "Personality Parade." April 1988. Copyright © Carol Copple, Ph. D.

Jabs, Carolyn. "On Best Behavior." November 1987. Copyright © Carolyn Jabs.

Katz, Debra Morgenstern. "It's How You Play the Game." September 1986. Copyright © Debra Morgenstern Katz.

Levitz, Barbara Gibbs. "Growing With Acceptance." July and September 1987.

Schwager, Istar, Ph.D. "Stages, Not Ages." March 1987.

Schwager, Istar, Ph.D. "What's So Funny?" March 1988.

Chapter Seven

Copple, Carol, Ph.D. "How to Explain Rain." October 1988. Copyright © Carol Copple, Ph.D.

Schwager, Istar, Ph.D. "Science: Early Explorations." June 1986.

Chapter Eight

Berman, Alice. "Making Music Together." April 1986. Copyright © Alice Berman.

Copple, Carol, Ph.D. "Ducks and Other Difficulties." May 1987. Copyright © Carol Copple, Ph.D.

Copple, Carol, Ph.D. "Dance to the Music." *Sesame Street Parents' Newsletter*. November 1982. Copyright © Carol Copple, Ph.D.

Thompson, Kathleen. "Fun and Games in an Art Museum." October 1986.

Chapter Nine

Alt, Anice M. "Choosing a Preschool." September 1986.

Schwager, Istar, Ph.D. "The Kindergarten Curriculum." September 1988.

Chapter Ten

Copple, Carol, Ph.D. "The First Goodbye." September 1985. Copyright © Carol Copple, Ph.D.

Chapter Eleven

Copple, Carol, Ph.D. "When a Child Is Gifted." September 1988. Copyright © Carol Copple, Ph.D.

Schwager, Istar, Ph.D. "Different Children, Different Gifts." September 1986.

Chapter Twelve

Cobb, Eulalia Benejam. "Classroom Conferences." September 1987. Copyright © Eulalia Benejam Cobb.

Series Introduction

• • • • • •

What do children need to learn about themselves and the world around them if they are to realize their potential? What can parents do to facilitate their children's emotional, physical, and intellectual growth?

For more than a generation, Children's Television Workshop, creators of *Sesame Street*, has asked these questions and has conducted extensive research to uncover the answers. We have gathered together some of the best minds in child development, health, and communication. We have studied what experts around the world are doing to nurture this generation. And, most important, we have worked with children and parents to get direct feedback on what it means to be a productive and fulfilled family member in our rapidly changing world. We recognize that there are no simple solutions to the inherent complexities of child rearing and that in most situations, there are no single answers that apply to all families. Thus, we do not offer a ''how-to'' approach to being a parent. Rather, we present facts where information will help each reader make appropriate decisions, and we offer strategies for finding solutions to the varied concerns of individual families.

The development of the CTW Family Living Series is a natural outgrowth of our commitment to share what we have learned with parents and others who care for today's children. It is hoped that the information presented here will make the job of parenting a little easier—and more fun.

Contents

• • • • • •

Preface by David Elkind   xix

A Few Words About Pronouns   xxv

PART I • The Joy of Learning   **1**

Introduction to Part I   3

CHAPTER ONE

Play and a Child's Learning Process   5

Motivation: The Inner Teacher   12

CHAPTER TWO

The Natural Course of Development   13

CHAPTER THREE

The Mind and Body Relationship   21

PART II • Enhancing the Process   **31**

Introduction to Part II   33

CHAPTER FOUR

Language—Speaking, Reading, and Writing   37

Going for a Walk with a Prereader   48

CHAPTER FIVE

Math—More than Numbers   51

CONTENTS

CHAPTER SIX
Social Skills   59
   It's How You Play the Game: Helping Your Child
      Develop Problem-Solving Strategies   64
   The Shy Child   67

CHAPTER SEVEN
Science—Early Explorations   89

CHAPTER EIGHT
The Arts   101
   Fun and Games in an Art Museum   106

PART III • Learning and Culture   **117**
Introduction to Part III   119

CHAPTER NINE
Early Childhood Education: What Can It Provide?   121

CHAPTER TEN
Getting Ready for Grade School   137

CHAPTER ELEVEN
Different Children, Different Gifts   155

CHAPTER TWELVE
How to Help Your Child Succeed in School   169

Afterword: Putting It All Together   177

Resources   183

Index   207

Preface

$\bullet \bullet \bullet \bullet \bullet \bullet$

Contemporary parents are excruciatingly aware of their parenting role. Books, magazines, newspaper articles, and TV programs bombard parents with the latest facts, theories, and fads regarding the best and most effective ways to rear children. Often the advice is contradictory. For example, some writers argue that "earlier is better" and that it is never too early to start children in reading, math, swimming, and music instruction. At the other extreme are those who argue that formal instruction should not be given until the child is eight or nine and that home schooling is the only effective antidote to the inadequacies of our public school system.

Parents today are confronted with a mind-dazzling array of choices regarding childrearing. To whom should they listen? Which advice should they follow? And what, a mother asked me after a lecture, if you are wrong? These are not easy questions. Nonetheless, the conflicts are not among professional educators but between the entrepreneurs—those willing to sell anything to parents—and the educational conservatives.

Caught between these two extremes, the professional educators—child psychologists, pediatricians, child psychiatrists, and child-development researchers—are in broad agreement as to what constitutes healthy childrearing and educational practices. This broad professional consensus is based on more than a century of child-development research as well as upon the accumulated wisdom of child-development professionals who have spent their lives working with children and their families. The research and the experts are quite consistent in the childrearing information and advice that they provide for parents.

Whether it is Benjamin Spock, T. Berry Brazelton, Bruno Bettleheim, Selma Fraiberg, Jean Piaget, or Erik Erikson, the message is fundamentally the same: Childhood is a stage of life, and like every other stage of life, it has it's own reasons and seasons. Childrearing and education is most healthy and effective when it takes the special qualities of childhood into account and adapts to them. Children are not miniature adults and are much more like us in their feelings than they are like us in their thoughts. And each of the experts, as well the research, encourages us to respect children's feelings while appreciating that their thinking is different than our own.

In many ways, this book emphasizes these two themes, namely, the uniqueness of childhood as a stage of life and respect for the child's point of view. Like the *Sesame Street Magazine* and the *Sesame Street* program, it provides a high level of professional expertise, presented in everyday language, with many well-chosen examples. But the book does much more than provide parents with useful information about the basics of human growth and development. Parents will find a hope chest of practical projects and activities that will enrich their childrearing in many different ways.

The importance of these projects and activities goes beyond their educational value. In my work, I find that many contemporary parents feel extremely guilty about their childrearing. This guilt may arise because they may fear they are placing a career ahead of their children, or because they believe they are doing the wrong thing, or the right thing at the wrong time. Parents today are perhaps too aware of all of their childrearing options as well as the risks of not doing the right thing at the right time. Freedom, as Erich Fromm, the psychoanalyst and influential author, pointed out long ago, is frightening and anxiety producing, and we often try to escape from it.

I find that many of today's parents attempt to do just that, escape from freedom. They have very busy schedules and not too much time to spend with their children. But the little time they do have to spend with their family, they use to rush their children from one lesson to another, or from one cultural activity to another, or to one social event after the other. While this may help resolve parental anxiety and guilt, it does little to foster the parent-child relationship or to enhance the child's overall growth.

What feels so right about the many projects and activities suggested in this book is that they accomplish what, I think, is our most important goal as parents: to share *ourselves* with our children. It is through sharing ourselves with our children that we convey not only our love, but our values, our principles and our ideals. It is the basis of all healthy and successful childrearing. If we have only a relatively small amount of time with our children, it is even more important that we engage in meaningful, shared activities. It is through sharing and enjoying common activities that we really get to know our children and they really get to know us. And it is through shared activities that we grow to like as well as to love our children and through which they grow to like as well as to love us.

What these joint projects achieve, and what formal lessons do not accomplish, is the enrichment and deepening of the child-parent relationship. But these projects and activities have many other benefits as well. Through these practical everyday activities, children learn important social skills such as paying attention, taking turns, and working cooperatively with another person. Such skills are basic prerequisites to working productively in a classroom setting. And, in the process of talking with our child, we not only enrich his or her vocabulary, we also give him or her the opportunity to practice language and to appreciate the nonverbal as well as the verbal facets of communication.

The projects and activities described in this book also help children learn about themselves. They come to know and, with our support and love, to accept some of their limitations as small persons in an adult-size and fabricated world. They learn the many things they can't do as well as the many things they can do. Yet they also come to see their limitations, not as permanent handicaps, but as challenges for the future. And when they do achieve new levels of development, they can leave the old ones with aplomb. As one third grader told me as he was putting up an Easter display for the younger children, "I don't believe in the Easter Bunny anymore!"

Concrete projects and activities also teach children a great deal of what might appear to be academic skills and knowledge, although it would really be a mistake to call them that. Children do not think in academic categories, and their learning of science, math, and chemistry is at the most basic level, but all important nonetheless. Cooking is a good example. In preparing soup children learn many different things. They learn measurement as they follow a recipe and add a spoonful of salt or a cup of sugar. These are easily perceived and understood measurements which do not presuppose an understanding of units—a kind of understanding which will come much later. Children also learn that boiling softens some things, like carrots and potatoes but hardens other things, like eggs. That is elementary chemistry.

Such activities are sometimes regarded as play. But play in

young children is never frivolous and just "having a good time." In early childhood, and perhaps throughout life, play is also a way in which we learn. Play is essentially generalization, going from the particular to the general, a fundamental learning process. When children play house they are generalizing from, and extending, their experiences at home. The same is true when they play store, or doctor's office and so on. Play is thus a sort of inductive process by means of which we are able to go from an immediate concrete instance to a generalization, a general form of the specific activity.

Children, of course, work as well as play. And, just as play is a kind of induction, work is a sort of deduction in which we go from the general to the particular. A child who is learning to tie his or her shoe, to hold a fork, or to write with a pencil is working. He or she is taking a very general skill and is applying it at a very specific and particular time and place. And whenever we do a job we are going from the general principles of our work or our profession to a special case or instance. Whether we are doctors or lawyers, crafts people or tradespeople, our work consists of bringing general principles to bear in specific cases.

So young children play and they work, and they learn through both types of activities. And, as the authors of this book make clear, discussions, projects and activities, not academic lessons, are the appropriate learning modes for young children. Long ago, Selma Fraiberg, who authored classic literature on child development, described early childhood as "the magic years." They are magic because children discover so many wondrous things about the world and about themselves. What is so nice about this book is that it helps parents appreciate, and contribute to, that special magic of early childhood.

DAVID ELKIND, Ph.D.

A Few Words About Pronouns

• • • • • •

"The child fell off *his* bike." Or how about "The child fell off *her* bike"? Then again we could say, "The child fell off *his or her* bike." How to deal with pronouns?

If you are a regular reader of *Sesame Street Magazine Parents' Guide,* you know that our policy is to alternate the use of gender-related pronouns. In one paragraph we say *his;* in the following one we use *her.* In a book, that specific policy is not quite as practical—there are just too many paragraphs—but it works in a general way, by alternating chapters.

PART I
......
The Joy of Learning

Introduction to Part I

• • • • • •

From the moment your child was born, she began to learn about this world. From that moment, too, you took on the role of teacher. The first lessons were simple ones: She found that a nipple led to the satisfaction of her hunger. She learned that being held felt good and that being wet was uncomfortable. Within the first weeks of life, she learned to recognize her parents' faces and voices as different from the faces and voices of other people. Soon, she lifted her head to get a better look at things; she grabbed for objects she wanted. Each of these new skills emerged according to nature's timetable, and you—watching and noting each new development—delighted in your new-born's progress.

As she grew from infancy to babyhood, the boundaries of her world enlarged. There were floors to crawl across, cabinet doors to open and close, blocks to stack, and food to squish in her fingers. There were also parents to observe, to learn from.

As the parents of each generation before them, today's parents take their role as teachers seriously. There is an important new element, however. Whereas parents once saw their teaching role primarily as models of moral behavior, instilling codes of proper conduct in their children, today's parents see themselves as having the additional responsibility of giving their children a "head start" on the competition—an academic and social edge that will prepare their kids for the twenty-first century. Understandably, many parents find this task daunting.

The good news is that children *want* to learn. In fact, the process can't be stopped. That leads to the following question: How can parents best encourage a child's natural love of learning? Perhaps the most important thing to remember is that each child develops at her own pace and that nature can't be rushed. Recognizing that childhood is a special phase of life, not simply a preparation for the ''real world'' of adulthood, will help protect both parents and children from the pressures of rushing through this special time. Childhood is a time for experimentation, a time for observation, a time for play. It is a time when a child learns who she is, not a time for judging herself (or being judged) for what she can do.

In this section, we discuss the ways that parents and children can share in the joys of learning. We'll also look at the ways that a child's physical, emotional, and intellectual development prepares her for learning and find out what child-development experts have discovered about how children learn.

CHAPTER ONE

• • • • • •

Play and a Child's Learning Process

This little piggy went to market,'' you cooed as you tickled your baby's big toe. He didn't understand a word you said, of course, but he *did* get your message. He learned to associate your smile, your voice, your gestures, and your playful touch with good times. He learned that his own happy response to your game playing brought more smiles from you. A wonderful circle was drawn.

Parents of infants are happily content to engage in play with their babies, to watch in wonder as their babies grow. Babies, doing what comes naturally to them, learn to lift their heads when their necks are strong enough, to turn themselves over when their muscles are ready, to reach for a toy when nature allows their eyes and hands to work together. Parents are there to facilitate each new stage of development, but, wisely, few parents try to rush their children through these early learning experiences. Nor do parents try to slow down this process. For now, the parent-child relationship is securely based on unconditional acceptance. The parents, in other words, follow their child's cues. Letting nature take the lead becomes harder as children begin to grow up, however. Parents may become concerned that their child is not progressing as he should—that is, not developing at the same pace as a neighbor's child or a sibling. They may want to intervene to help their child "catch up." Then they wonder, "What kind of intervention is appropriate?"

Learning: An Active Process That Begins with Play

Water is wet. It can be poured from one container into another. You can make a terrific splash with it.

These are things that a one-year-old learns through experience. If anyone tried to teach him these laws of nature through words or pictures alone, the concepts wouldn't mean much. But ten minutes of bathtub play will make this lesson clear.

For all people, learning is an active process. For children, hands-on experience is the prime route to discovering what the world around them is like. All the academic learning, all the social skills, all the intellectual and emotional growth that parents hope their children will enjoy begin with a child's poking and prying into his physical world. A parent's role in this process is to provide the tools and the encouragement for the experimentation; in other words, to allow a child to do what comes naturally—to play.

By playing with pots and pans, for instance, a toddler learns to match assorted containers to their same-size lids. By mixing blue and yellow paints, a five-year-old learns the properties of the color green. By building a house of cards, a seven-year-old learns some principles of architecture.

While much of this spontaneous play may appear haphazard and random, it is, in fact, organized around the needs of the child who initiates the play. At each stage of his development, the child is using the things around him to lead him to discoveries he is ready to make. These discoveries, which kids are constantly revising and refining, serve as the foundation for much of the learning that will take place later on.

The child's self-initiated learning occurs with or without

parental involvement, though parental involvement can affect the process. When parents step in and take the lessons of play beyond the child's level of interest or ability, they can inadvertently turn their child off to further experimentation. On the other hand, when they join in as supportive coexplorers, taking the lead from their child, they can enhance the play experience. While watching a child build a block tower, for instance, a parent can supply additional props, such as paper-towel tubes, to add to the structure. Or the parent can ask leading questions, such as, ''What do you think would happen if you put this big block on top of that little block?'' to encourage the child to consider what works and what doesn't. By showing enthusiasm, without taking over the child's game, parents send the message that the *process* of play is important and that the child is engaged in an appropriate activity.

Creating the Setting for Play

Providing enthusiasm is the best foundation for encouraging your child's natural gift for learning. But that's not all that parents can offer.

Children also need age-appropriate playthings—objects that provide for safe, happy times; that they can use in a variety of ways; and that stretch their imaginations just enough, but not beyond their reach.

Toys need not be labeled ''educational'' to be appropriate. A teddy bear to whom a child can tell his woes or to whom he can pretend to read a story helps a child develop his coping skills and his language skills. A cardboard box that can be a spaceship one moment and a playhouse the next helps a child to develop his imagination as well as his physical skills as he climbs in and out.

Kids also need unstructured materials such as modeling clay, sand, and water so they can experiment with various textures. They need structured materials such as blocks, puzzles, and board games to encourage them to develop plans and strategies. They need props for imaginative play—anything from dress-up clothes to model villages. And they need safe, comfortable places to play, places where neither they nor their parents have to worry about breaking the china or spilling paints on the rug. At home, that means providing as much space as possible where children can have (relatively) free rein. Play clothes, too, should be comfortable and casual enough that a child can sit on the floor or tromp around outdoors without anyone worrying that his clothes stay neat and clean.

Every child also needs opportunities for balance in his play. He needs time outdoors to use large muscles, to climb and run, and to be able to shout as loudly as he wants. He needs time indoors to draw with crayons, to play with puzzles, and to listen to music. He needs time to play with friends, time to play with parents, and time to play alone. Most importantly, he needs time to grow up, free of the pressure to perform beyond his natural capabilities.

First Friendships: Kids Teaching Kids

Besides a place to play and objects with which to play, children, of course, need playmates. The learning that occurs when children play with other children differs somewhat from the learning that occurs when they are alone because it is only by spending time with playmates that children learn about social interaction among peers. As in every other area of learning development, the child's major task is determining what those lessons are.

Toddlers, for example, tend to play *alongside* one another, often focusing on different activities. This side-by-side experience prepares them for future friendships. Preschoolers, however, begin to learn the give-and-take that characterizes more grown-up social interaction. Their developing maturity allows them, for the first time, to understand the basics of sharing. By age four or five, the ability to see another person's point of view begins to take hold, leading to an understanding of such social graces as waiting one's turn. By age six or seven, children begin to understand that games' rules are based on common consent. As they pass through each stage of development, however, their behavior doesn't always reflect their most advanced thinking. Five-year-olds, for instance, may still occasionally balk at waiting their turns. Like other areas of learning, social learning progresses in fits and starts, and kids will, quite naturally, regress from time to time.

Children benefit from having friends of all ages. Younger children learn to stretch their reach by playing with older kids. Older kids can learn nurturance and develop a sense of pride by playing with younger kids. But friendships between children of the same age hold special benefits. Particularly after the age of three, peer friendships give children a chance to discover that another person's claim to attention, possessions, and turns on the rocking horse may be just as compelling and valid as their own. It also gives them an opportunity to work out these differences with a person equally matched in size, emotional maturity, and vocabulary. With some adult prompting when needed, children do a lot of negotiating with one another, and these discussions help them form a more balanced view of other people's needs, feelings, and thoughts as distinct from their own.

Incidental Learning: Children Learn from What They See

A great part of what children learn is never "taught" to them but is learned incidentally. Children notice how the important people around them spend their time, talk to each other, and treat other people. They discover what makes their parents' faces light up and what makes them grouchy. They notice how other children dress. They form some idea, sometimes as early as age four or five, about what's cool and what's silly. Television and influences from the neighborhood and culture at large are all incorporated into a child's view of the world. And most of this learning is not in the form of formal "lessons" but occurs informally and incidentally. Attitudes about sex roles and ethnic stereotypes, achievement, material possessions, and violence all abound, in various forms, in our culture. While it is neither possible nor even desirable for parents to protect their children from the larger world, adults do need to take some responsibility for helping children interpret the very complex environment in which we all live.

The most important interpreters of the world, of course, are a child's parents, and the most important teaching parents do occurs when they act as role models, teaching by example, not by words alone.

Your child will notice whether *you* buckle your seatbelt, are selective in your television viewing, and eat your vegetables. By the same token, your child will be aware of how you handle your disappointments and anger, how you respond to demands, and how you unwind and relax.

It helps for parents to be aware that their actions are constantly setting examples for their children about what *really* matters. The incidental lessons can be extended, of course. A parent who is proud to see a three-year-old put away his toys can say so. If you are delighted with the way your six-year-old helps his younger brother do a puzzle, your positive comments will provide a powerful message that you endorse his actions wholeheartedly.

Praise helps provide children with direction by conveying to them what activities and actions parents approve of. Encouragement, a form of positive reinforcement, is an important tool parents can use to help guide their children toward learning healthy and productive behavior—everything from cooperation to consideration, from neatness to inventiveness to good eating habits. Praise and encouragement are more potent than punishment, because they identify for a child what you would like him to do, thereby helping him learn. At the same time, praise helps give a child a sense of pride and accomplishment. It is definitely a win-win situation.

Teaching the Whole Child

Each child is a unique individual with many dimensions. In understanding how young children learn, it is essential to recognize that the emotional and social aspects of a child's being cannot be separated from the physical or the intellectual aspects. A child with a strong sense of emotional well-being, a child with high self-esteem and confidence, will approach new challenges with curiosity and optimism.

Mastery of the physical and social worlds helps build a child's feelings of worth. And intellectual involvement helps a child extend his ability to cope in all the other spheres. All aspects of a child effect one another; no dimension can ever be approached in isolation. Parents are a child's first and primary teachers. Their early influence plays a major role in helping a child develop a healthy and positive self-image and in encouraging a child to enjoy fully the fun and excitement of learning.

• •

Motivation: The Inner Teacher

Underlying most voluntary human activity, including learning, is the issue of motivation. Children start off liking to learn *if* what they are learning has meaning to them. What makes learning meaningful? For learning to be meaningful it must be connected in some way to important emotional, intellectual, social, or physical challenges a child is grappling with at the moment. If a child is developmentally ready and if what is learned is useful to the child in some way, then that child will find learning exciting. It is fascinating for a baby to discover that objects can be dropped and retrieved. A toddler feels great power in being able to master the fundamentals of speech. And a six-year-old who can sign his name on a drawing knows he's at the gateway to a new world of written communication. Each of these children wants to learn and is excited about expanding and extending his mastery of the world. Each is propelled from within by his own interests, curiosity, and desire for competence.

• •

CHAPTER TWO

· · · · · ·

The Natural Course of Development

How can parents know what their child is capable of at various ages and stages?

The first step is to observe her. What does she do with ease? What does she struggle with? What captures her attention? What bores her? Is she happiest when she engages in boisterous physical activity or when she's quietly observing a bug on the sidewalk? Does a challenging problem cause her to work harder at finding a solution or does she become too frustrated to remain interested? Recognizing where your child is right now can help you determine what her needs are right now. If a fifty-piece puzzle is so frustrating that it's abandoned, it cannot provide a compelling or fun learning experience. Perhaps a twenty-piece puzzle would be more appropriate. Or perhaps a nonjudgmental suggestion from you to try a particular strategy might ease her frustration enough to reignite her enthusiasm. The point is to help the child find a level of comfort before expecting her to go off into unfamiliar territory.

When you observe your child, of course, you do so through the prism of your own feelings. Reaching beyond your own observations can help. What do teachers and day-care workers observe about her social and academic development? What does her pediatrician think of her physical growth? How does she relate to her peers? Is she able to do many of the things that her friends can do? The observations of others, combined with your own observations, can help round out the picture.

The Role of Nature

Recognizing that nature plays a major role in development is essential, too. No matter how your child seems to compare to other children, it is important to remember that each child is progressing according to her own inner timetable. Each child's natural unfolding of abilities and skills sets the stage for each new learning experience, and no amount of pushing can force a child to learn something that she is not yet ready to learn. This progression of physical, intellectual, and social skills unfolds at about the same time and in the same order in just about all children, whether they live in Kansas or Kenya, in Peoria or Paris.

Parents and teachers who understand nature's role are freed to support children's growth rather than try to upset its natural course. While there are, of course, those who say that teaching reading or math to two-year-olds is beneficial, the evidence does not support their claims. Certainly, some toddlers can be prodded into reading or doing simple addition, but at what cost to their sense of worth? At its worst, making such demands on young children can lead them to believe that they are valued primarily for their ability to perform. At its best, structured teaching for children this young is fruitless.

In one often-quoted experiment conducted in 1929 by researchers Arnold Gesell and Helen Thompson at Yale University, one child in a set of twins was trained to walk up and down stairs. Not surprisingly, the untrained twin became an equally adept stair walker, without any training, when she had naturally developed the necessary physical coordination. The researchers found that all the time and effort spent in instructing one twin in the art of walking up and down stairs made no difference. And who knows what other, more appropriate, activities the "trained" twin might have engaged in during those instruction sessions?

While abilities may emerge at different times in different children, development follows a fairly consistent pattern. Much of what we know today about the natural developmental stages of children is based on the work of Swiss psychologist Jean Piaget, who began his work in the early part of this century.

Piaget started out as a biologist, but his interest turned to psychology. His training in the physical sciences held fast, however. Like a biologist, he saw infants as organisms who adapt to a new environment—the world.

Piaget saw two ways infants could adapt: They could use what they already knew to make sense of new experiences. Or, where that was too hard, they could change their picture of the world and their ways of thinking. Piaget called the first approach *assimilation* and the second, *accommodation*.

For instance, a newborn can make sucking movements with her lips. By applying that action to something in the environment—a breast or the nipple of a bottle—she learns to suck for food. Piaget would say that she *assimilates* the nipple to the sucking motion. If the nipple's too big, however, she learns to purse her lips differently. In other words, she changes her approach to the world in order to deal with the new object. She *accommodates*.

Assimilation and accommodation, accepting knowledge and responding to knowledge, are the two basic approaches people use to make sense of new experience—to learn—according to Piaget. These are approaches that persist throughout our lives. But in another sense, said Piaget, we learn differently as we grow older. We work our way through four stages of development, learning at each stage according to our ability.

Piaget's Four Stages: The Development of Thought

Stage One: Sensorimotor. From birth to age two, children are in the *sensorimotor* stage. The kind of action we usually call *thinking* hasn't begun. A child is learning to use her body, learning to coordinate actions, learning the effect her body can have on the world. She's learning that objects in the world react to her—plates drop and break, Mom and Dad smile and change diapers, mirrors reflect.

By six or seven months, she is developing goals—reaching for what she wants, crawling toward destinations. By the end of her first year, she's becoming aware that objects still exist even when they're out of sight. Soon, she starts to experiment. She develops mental ideas of objects and actions. Before long, she can anticipate what will happen when she bangs her spoon on Dad's head.

Stage Two: Preoperational. Piaget placed children from age two to age seven in the *preoperational* stage. They think, he said, but their conclusions are often wrong. A child at this stage is learning to speak, but she often uses words incorrectly. Much of her speech, said Piaget, is directed toward herself, not toward others.

A preoperational child doesn't quite understand how the world works, but she's trying. She develops her own version of the laws of nature—ways in which she believes the world works. For example, in a classic Piagetian experiment, a researcher empties a test tube full of water into a low, flat dish. The water looks different, so a pre-operational child believes there's less water in the dish than there had been in the test tube.

In similar studies, Piaget investigated children's notions of weight, length, quantity, weather, astronomy, and game rules. Children at the preoperational stage, he found, are often confused by the appearance of change. Thus, they have difficulty considering multiple points of view.

Stage Three: Concrete Operations. By the time a child enters the stage of *concrete operations*—usually between the ages of seven and eleven—she's able to put those multiple points of view together and make sense of them. The child has begun to understand that a clay ball, when flattened into a pancake, still has the same amount of clay. She's also becoming expert at classifying similar objects into groups, arranging them in ordered series (small to big, fat to skinny, etc.), and counting them. More and more, she uses speech to communicate with others. More and more, too, she can follow rules and understand another's point of view.

Stage Four: Formal Operations. The fourth and last stage, *formal operations*, begins at about age eleven, said Piaget. In the formal-operations stage, the child is able to solve problems in her head, unlike the concrete-operational child, who needs to consider physical objects. The adolescent, for example, can imagine different possible outcomes from the same event. She can sensibly explain new information, develop ways to solve problems, suggest possibilities, and draw logical conclusions. She can develop hypotheses about a problem and understand various solutions. She's ready, in short, to think scientifically.

Piaget worked by watching children as they tried to solve problems. He watched his own children as infants. Later, he watched children at play. He presented them with problems, watched them solve them, and asked them questions. Studying children in many situations, he and his followers concluded that all children pass through all the stages in the same order. Some move along more quickly, some lag behind by months or even years, but everyone makes the same journey.

Today, Piaget remains as the greatest influence on modern notions of how children think. Every teacher, every child psychologist, everyone who studies children studies his work. And his work is the basis of ongoing research, as psychologists try to improve our understanding of the way thinking develops.

Recently, some psychologists have begun to take a new look at Piaget's four stages of development. For example, some wonder whether, contrary to Piaget's observation, young children can indeed understand multiple points of view. Piaget determined that they could not do so on the basis of many experiments similar to the one in which he asked children to compare water in a test tube with water in a shallow dish. For instance, he would line up two sticks so that a child could see that they were identical in length. Then he'd ask the child, "Are they the same length?" When the child said "yes," Piaget would slide one stick in his hand so that one of its ends stuck out past the end of the other stick. "Are they the same length?" he'd ask again. A six-year-old would change her response and say "no."

The child, Piaget concluded, couldn't use all the information available. She concentrated on one end, the protruding end, and ignored the empty space at the other end that evened things out. Piaget concluded that she couldn't use reason to understand that a simple action would restore the original set-up.

In the early 1970s Susan Rose and Marion Blank tried a slightly different version of Piaget's experiment. They asked, ''Are the sticks the same length?'' just once—*after* changing the arrangement—and they got a different result. Many more children seemed to understand that the sticks, though they looked different, were the same length.

Was Piaget wrong? Not exactly. But Rose and Blank believe he ignored a significant aspect of the situation. By asking the question twice, he signaled the children in his experiments to look for a change. The children may have known all along that the sticks were the same length, but they wanted to acknowledge the highlighted change. They were responding to the context of the question, not to the evidence in front of them.

Other post-Piaget researchers are investigating children's language; perhaps, they suggest, children *can* think more powerfully than Piaget believed, but they simply don't have the language to express their thoughts. Still others zero in on Piaget's contention that development, though it may progress at a different pace in each child, is continuous and unvarying.

One persistent question is: How does learning happen? In other words, what causes thought to develop? Piaget, as we've seen, believed that the workings of the mind itself push and pull it along to new ways of working and that each person's mind assimilates, or takes in new knowledge, and accommodates, or changes ways of thinking to meet new challenges. This mental exercise builds new powers of thought.

Perhaps, say some thinkers—but perhaps Piaget underemphasized a critical factor. As she grows, a child's senses become more acute and her brain more powerful. Some achievements in the development of thought may be a function not just of a child's experience but of her evolving physical equipment, as discussed in the next chapter.

CHAPTER THREE

• • • • • •

The Mind and Body Relationship

Touch a rock, a flower, or a hard-boiled egg and what happens? Nothing. But touch a spider, a tiger, or a baby, and it responds. Animals have the remarkable ability to take in information from the world around them, to make their own kind of sense out of it, and to respond—to skitter away, to snap, to coo.

Some animals have an even more remarkable ability: They remember. They learn. Of all the species that are able to learn, the most remarkable are humans. All told, we sense, we interpret, we respond, and we learn more skillfully and more flexibly than any other creature on earth. That's because we have the most sophisticated equipment for gathering, sorting, and storing information ever known—the human nervous system.

When you see a red flower and breathe in its scent, your nervous system is working. When you combine information—the color red, the sweet scent, the arrangement of delicate petals—and conclude that the flower is a rose, your nervous system is working. When you feel the prick of a thorn and—without a thought—raise your thumb to your mouth to ease the pain, your nervous system's at work. And when you remember to be more careful the next time you pluck a rose, that's your nervous system, too.

The nervous system of a child is nearly the same as the nervous system of an adult—nearly, but not quite. Like the rest of the child's body, it's still growing. That's the physical basis of the psychological development we looked at in chapter 2. Throughout the first years of life, the nervous system develops according to a natural timetable, becoming ready to take on new challenges like walking and speech.

Experience may help the system along. Some biologists believe that experience prompts physical changes in the brain. For instance, the experience of learning to count may physically change the brain to make new learning—like learning to add or multiply—possible.

There's more to the nervous system than the brain, however. The system also includes built-in sensors all over the body that pick information up and pass it along. It includes a system of one-way streets, highways, and superhighways that move information back and forth from the skin, muscles, and other organs to the spinal cord and the brain. And it includes chemicals and electrical pulses that zip information along those nerve roadways in amazingly short spans of time.

The nervous system is our tool kit for learning, whether learning to tie a shoelace or learning to design a spaceship. The brain, the "control center" of the nervous system, is not fully developed at birth.

While the *brainstem*, which is located at the base of the brain and is the part responsible for such fundamental life functions as breathing and heart rate, is on duty as soon as a baby is born, the *cortex*, the part responsible for higher human abilities, located at the very top of the brain, matures relatively late in a baby's life.

As different parts of the brain develop, the baby becomes ready to crawl, walk, speak, read—to learn. The pace of development seems to be set largely by the baby's built-in timetable. Experience plays a role, but experience can't rush the process. That's why no one-year-old brain is ready to read. No child can leap ahead of his thinking equipment.

Experience and Growth:
An Unbeatable Team

How do experience and physical growth work together? The development of vision is a useful example of this crucial, complicated interaction. Visual development starts with experience. The first light entering a newborn's eye triggers the process, sending a message to his brain. That activates the part of his cortex devoted to vision. Visual perception begins.

The quality of this first perception is limited by the baby's built-in timetable. The equipment isn't fully formed. The eye still has trouble focusing. In fact, scientists at the Massachusetts Institute of Technology have determined that even at ten weeks, babies see so poorly that they could be declared legally blind.

The newborn's range of vision is narrow, too. Later in life, each eye will see a full 90 degrees. Now the range is only 30 degrees. That's why babies move their heads from side to side to see. By toddlerhood, they move only their eyes.

As the baby grows older, he develops new abilities. He's able to distinguish more visual details. He's able to coordinate his two eyes. At around four months, he's able to perceive depth—to see in three dimensions.

These aspects of visual development depend on experience as well as biology. The brain becomes ready for the next developmental step according to its biological timetable, but without experience, it may not take the step. For instance, if one of an infant's eyes remains covered for very long, the infant may grow up blind in that eye—simply because the eye was denied experience. In normal development, with both eyes open, both send messages to the cortex, and as the cortex develops, it comes to expect messages from both eyes. But if one eye is kept closed, the nerve pathway from that eye to the cortex has no messages to carry, and before long, the cortex starts to ignore that pathway. It looks to the other eye's pathway for all of its information. When the closed eye reopens and starts sending messages, it's in trouble; the messages just won't register on the cortex. The eye itself may work but, ignored by the brain, it's effectively blind.

Despite what is known about the connection between physical development and experience, no one can say with certainty how any particular experience will affect mental growth. On the other hand, no one can deny that, generally speaking, experience is as important for the growth of a healthy brain as physical exercise is for the growth of strong muscles.

Many experts in child development have sketched out categories of experience and experience-rich environments that may foster the development of a normal, healthy nervous system. But the fact is that there is no recipe. Babies are human beings, and each human being is unique. Each body grows differently, and each brain grows differently.

Unique from the Very Start

A baby's very first experience will send him down a path that only he will ever travel. But his uniqueness is there even before his first experience. It's sealed in a code that scientists have only begun to understand—a marvelous arrangement of just four chemical substances. Those four chemicals make up a different blueprint for each human being: that individual's DNA molecules.

DNA is a chemical code that determines who we are,

from a biological point of view. The code expresses itself from birth, in features like the colors of a baby's eyes and hair. But it also holds surprises, revealed with the passage of time. In a few years, the cute button nose may grow long and noble. At puberty, the entire body will take on a new shape. Years later, hair may grow coarse or thin. Just because a characteristic is hereditary doesn't mean it's permanent. Change, too, is sealed in the genetic code.

Some inherited characteristics can be spotted even by a stranger. These include physical characteristics like skin tone, hair color, or the shape of a baby's eyes. Other, subtler expressions of the genetic code are apparent to people who know the baby well, like his parents. These characteristics include personality traits.

A Personality All His Own

Once, it was thought that a baby's personality was determined solely by his genetic background. Then the pendulum swung in the opposite direction as experts claimed that environment alone determined personality. More recent research suggests that there are both environmental and genetically determined influences which form the complex web of human character.

Personality takes shape through the interaction of inborn tendencies and real-world experience. From the beginning, it takes experience to activate an inherited tendency. Later in life, experience can change a child's personality.

In fact, research shows that an infant's personality may change quite a bit by the time he reaches school age. Many types of experience can be involved. A physical problem in infancy, such as a temporary allergy, might pass, allowing the child to refocus his attention away from bodily discomfort to the world outside himself. The response of caregivers to a baby's behavior can have an effect, too. In general, it seems, children tend to adopt personality characteristics that society values. In the United States, for example, a respectful but independent personality is widely valued. Some researchers have found that in the United States, inhibited children become more outgoing as they grow older, while extremely aggressive children often become less aggressive. In cultures where the group is valued above the individual, however, children will, by and large, adapt their personalities differently, becoming more docile than they might otherwise be, for instance.

Because change in personality is possible—even likely—many experts warn parents away from slotting children into categories like ''hard to handle,'' ''rambunctious,'' or ''passive.'' It's more helpful to recognize that each child is a unique individual and to respond to each child's needs in a thoughtful, caring way.

Personality and Learning

Personality, naturally, affects learning. A short attention span, a tendency to be easily distracted or frustrated, or a shy, inhibited approach to new activities can make it more difficult for a child to grapple with new learning situations. An eager, enthusiastic outlook, a tendency to focus on the task at hand, or a flexible nature can ease a child's struggle with even the thorniest learning problem.

The relationship between personality and learning goes both ways. Since humans, young and old, like to learn, experiences that are pleasant and successful can enhance

THE MIND AND BODY RELATIONSHIP

self-esteem, thus inspiring us and invigorating our learning. Repeated frustrating attempts to learn, on the other hand, can breed pessimism, a negative self-image, and a diminished willingness to take chances. Failure and the expectation of failure can follow each other in a vicious circle. Keeping in mind that children develop at their own pace can free adults from trying to rush the learning process and can free children to follow their own clocks without fear of an alarm going off. That doesn't mean, however, that parents can't help their children develop tactics for learning.

Tactics for Learning

Let's start with newborns. They have only a few learning tactics: their senses. If a bit of information can't be seen, smelled, heard, tasted, or felt, no newborn can be aware of it, much less learn it. As we saw earlier, it takes time for a child's powers of perception to develop enough to make sense of new information. Little by little, babies develop new learning tactics. For instance, at some point around his fifth or sixth month, a child begins to notice that he can affect the world. His actions, he finds, cause a reaction in other people and things. When he cries, his parents come. When he lets go of his bottle, it falls to the floor and makes a lovely noise. As his memory improves, the child is able to compare new experiences with old ones. He doesn't just react to the bottle-dropping noise; he expects it to happen. He anticipates the results of his actions. He begins to experiment. He discovers a time-honored learning tactic: trial and error.

Through trial and error, the baby learns not only about the world around him but also about his own body. He trains his own muscles—in his face, his arms, his legs—and that's another important kind of learning.

Hearing and understanding language are learning tactics, too—new ways of taking in information. As a baby's brain develops and tries to make sense of the noises coming out of his parents' mouths, he begins to understand language. He'll be a teenager before he's reached his full capacity to understand and use words (for instance, to distinguish and choose between words with similar meanings, to solve problems with language), but he's making a start.

Before long, he tries to produce language himself—to speak. The moment he asks his first question, he has taken charge of yet another learning tactic. Now the tactics come fast and furious, becoming more and more sophisticated. Questions become more specific. Once, the child was satisfied asking "whats" and "hows": "What's this thing?" "What is it for?" "How do you do it?" "How does it work?" Now he asks "whys": "Why did you do it that way?" "Why don't dogs have kittens?"

With help and direction from adults or older children, the child begins to use his vision skills and his growing language skills together in a new learning tactic—reading. He sees little black marks and trains his brain to sort them into distinct letters, words, and sentences. Reading is, at first, a conscious task. With practice, it becomes a virtually automatic pathway to new learning.

Just as the eyes—long used to see the world—are now used to read, so the muscles of the arm—long used to explore the physical world, to stack blocks, push balls, and open doors—are being trained to write. The child is working to control fine movements of his fingers, hand, and arm, guiding a pencil across a piece of paper to reproduce those little black marks he's just begun to read. Writing leads to new ways of thinking, organizing, and expressing thoughts.

There are other tactics, too. There are running and jumping, throwing and catching, clapping, digging, and tying, to name just a few. Some will help a child play baseball, jacks, or chess. Some will help him learn piano, dancing, or karate. He'll learn to combine tactics. In a few years, he'll start to take notes while reading. He'll jot down finger positions to help learn chords on the guitar. He'll study a video to improve the muscle movements that make up his tennis swing. Combining tactics can help him learn more things more quickly.

While children will progress according to their inner clocks and their innate abilities, parents *can* enhance the learning process. In the next section, we discuss enjoyable, stress-free ways of promoting your child's natural desire to learn.

PART II

......

Enhancing the Process

Introduction to Part II

• • • • • •

As discussed in Part I, much of what children can and can't do at a particular age is determined by neurological and other maturational factors. Just as babies learn to crawl at different ages, children mature at different rates throughout childhood and adolescence.

Parents often become worried when they see a neighbor's child excel in a skill their own child has not yet mastered. They wonder if they should put a little pressure on their child so that she can "catch up."

By rushing kids into activities they're not ready for, however, parents may unintentionally make it more difficult for their children to succeed in those activities later on, when the time is right. And just as kids of the same age are often at very different developmental levels, within the same child, there may be many levels operating at the same time. In other words, development is often lopsided; it occurs faster in some areas than in others. The precocious musician may be the last to tie her shoes, for example. Or the agile atheletē may have trouble telling time. Over time, too, these discrepancies often shift.

It's important to give kids leeway in our expectations of them. When children are tired or ill or experiencing stress, they often act in more babyish ways than usual. When changes occur in a child's regular routines, it can be stressful, even if the changes are positive. For instance, a move to a new house, the birth of a sibling, or starting a new school are all likely to evoke behavior in your child reminiscent of an earlier era in her life. Temporary lapses are quite normal. Even seemingly small changes in your child's life can sometimes wreak havoc. It's important to be patient and supportive. If you have any serious concern about your child's development, it may be a good idea to check with your pediatrician for his or her advice. And if your child is in school, it can help to talk to the teacher about how she is handling each new stage of academic and social growth.

One of the best ways you as a parent can encourage development without pushing is to take the lead from your child. See what new activities your child gravitates to in nursery school or at a friend's house. Give your child time to practice the activities that she is working on mastering, whether it's doing puzzles or going down the slide. Keep a few toys and games around that your child can grow into, as well as some things that she has basically outgrown. Having old, familiar toys around is comforting, and children play with the same toys in different ways at various stages of development. And having new, challenging toys around gives children a chance to experiment with new skills without necessarily having to play with the toys in the way intended.

Exposure to interesting experiences is one of the best ways to help enrich your child's life, no matter what her age. Trips to the zoo are great, but don't be surprised if the most exciting part of the trip for your child is the animal feeder, the lost balloon, or the sparrow drinking water from the hippos' trough. Also keep in mind that experiences don't have to be exotic for children to find them wonderful. A walk through the park with a jar of bubbles or an afternoon doing the laundry with Dad may be the highlight of a child's week.

Ultimately, the best experience we can offer our children is the comfort of knowing that we respect and value them for what they are. In the chapters that follow, we suggest fun, nonstressful activities to help you develop your child's natural instinct for learning.

CHAPTER FOUR

• • • • • •

Language—Speaking, Reading, and Writing

It is an amazing process to witness—the transformation of a gurgling infant into a person with whom you can hold a conversation. At three months, he's crying and cooing; at twelve months, he's able to say a word or two; just a few years later, he has a vocabulary of hundreds of words and has virtually mastered the complex language system. For parents and language specialists alike, language development has long been something of a mystery. But today researchers are shedding some light on this seemingly magical process.

The story of how the ability to communicate develops does not begin with the first word, but at birth. A newborn isn't trying to communicate. He cries by reflex, because he's hungry or in pain. But his cries get results. Less dramatic sounds like cooing and babbling get results, too. Adults smile, talk, and touch him, and he continues making sounds. A primitive sort of dialogue is established as parents make further efforts toward communication, responding to the child's actions whenever they can, as this conversation demonstrates:

FATHER (rubbing baby's stomach): Hi, fella. Let's have a little smile.

INFANT: (yawns)

FATHER: You're a sleepy little guy today, huh?

37

INFANT: (kicks legs energetically)

FATHER: (following baby's gaze in the direction of the window fan): Hey, now you're excited. Oh, you see the fan.

A major transition takes place as a child begins to understand that adults can help him get what he wants. Nine-month-old Kenny, for example, was sitting on his mother's lap as Mom made Kenny's toy bear perform a dance just beyond Kenny's reach. After several tries to reach the bear, Kenny pulled his mother's arm to get at the bear. A month later, in a similar situation, Kenny simply touched his mother's arm to signal that he wanted his toy.

The shift from arm pulling to communication by touch alone is an important one: Now, Kenny is making a reasoned request. A few months later, Kenny makes his first attempts to use words for the same purposes previously achieved nonverbally. Rather than gesturing to get what he wants, he now mimics the sound of the word *bear*. Mom uses the context of the situation and her knowledge of Kenny to interpret the utterance: "Oh, you want your toy bear?" Kenny has entered the world of verbal communication.

Learning Language

Does Kenny know the word *bear* and its meaning? Not exactly. Learning the meaning of a word involves more than just associating a sound with an object. Suppose Kenny's experience with the word *ball* comes from hearing family members use it to refer to the small red rubber ball in his toy chest. When someone says, "Where's your ball?" or,

"Ball?" Kenny can find it in a clutter of toys. His proud family concludes that he understands the meaning of *ball*. Well, he does and he doesn't. Kenny has made a link between a sound and an object in the world. He has grasped that one refers to the other. This understanding is essential for language.

On the other hand, what *ball* initially means to Kenny is not what it means to an adult. He may use it only to name his own small red rubber ball. Or he may apply it to a variety of objects—a plastic bead, an orange, perhaps the head of a snowman—while failing to include his brother's football. He has yet to learn what the grown-up world includes in the category *ball*.

At around the age of eighteen to twenty months, children take another giant step forward: They begin to put words together. Psychologists have found that the word order young children use when creating their first sentences is quite consistent and, in fact, follows the basic rules used by adult speakers. A child will say "Adam sit" to describe what he is doing; he will not say "Sit Adam." All over the world, children begin talking about very similar things, too. They first use words either to get more of something ("More cookie" or "More read") or to disagree ("No bed"). They also talk about people doing things ("Mommy eat"), the location of objects ("Book floor"), or the appearance of people and things ("Hi, doggie").

The Preschool Years

Language at age two is definitely a no-frills proposition: no word endings, no prepositions, no articles—none of the little bits of information that clarify and refine meaning. By the time a child is two-and-a-half, his skeletal sentence begins to fill out. As he begins to use word endings—usually by age three—we get an inside look at the child's mental process of learning language. By this age, he is no longer a mere imitator. Instead, he's an inventor, as this conversation between a preschooler and his mother demonstrates:

CHILD: My teacher holded the baby rabbits and we patted them.
MOTHER: Did you say your teacher held the baby rabbits?
CHILD: Yes.
MOTHER: What did you do when she held them?
CHILD: When she holded the baby rabbits, we patted them.

This child is following a "rule" about language that he has learned only recently. A year ago, when he was still at the mimicking stage, he would have used the word *held* appropriately. But now he has learned that past-tense verbs are formed with *-ed* endings; he isn't ready to learn exceptions to that rule, and his mother's repeated modeling of the irregular verb form *held* does not ruffle him in the least.

Attention to patterns of language shows up again and again in children's spontaneous language play when they are on their own. A toddler who's putting on his socks might recite a list of rhyming words: "socks, blocks, clocks, tocks." Or he might practice word patterns: "Whose socks? My socks. My red socks. Not my blue socks."

Learning to Communicate

In children's preschool and school years, their friends and siblings help them progress in language development and communication. Young children are relatively poor at taking the listener's perspective into account when they talk. A child who is building a roadway out of blocks announces,

"I need more." An adult will tend to look at what the child has done so far and provide the appropriate blocks. A peer will be less likely to do so. He will pass along the first blocks that come to hand or something else entirely—trucks or dolls. These message failures provide feedback to the young speaker. With development, he will be able to make greater use of this feedback and to anticipate problems in communication before he speaks.

Increased ability to consider the listener's viewpoint appears more and more as the child grows. Experiences with peers—joking, negotiating, arguing, collaborating—play an important role in the development of language and communication skills throughout childhood and adolescence.

How Parents Participate

Language is not something parents set out to teach. Their greatest contribution lies in their desire to interact with children. Through their parents' attempts, children become partners in communication.

The following are some important points that may be helpful for you to remember as you help pave the way for language acquisition:

- **The best way for you to relate to your child is to speak naturally,** leaving it to your child to copy your language pattern as he will. Children learn from language models, but they learn at their own pace. From the speech they hear, children select the materials they need for development.

- **Correcting your child's speech usually has no effect—or a negative effect.** Children who are just learning language aren't familiar with all the rules—especially inconsistencies in those rules—as the *held/holded* dialogue shows. Double negatives, too, present a problem for children who are just learning that certain words mean *no.* ''I don't want none,'' communicates the message very well for a child. Suggesting ''I don't want *any*'' to your child won't do much good. Instead of feeling frustrated, you should be patient and appreciative of your child's naturally paced growth.

• **Subtle rephrasing can help your child grasp the intricacies of language.** Studies have found that when parents respond to what a child says by restating the child's own words, the child's acquisition of language is promoted. For example:

> CHILD: Truck go away.
> ADULT: Yes, the truck is going away. Where is it going, I wonder?

The adult's first sentence is closely related to the child's but provides something additional, in this case the article *the* and the progressive verb form *is going.* Researchers think restating helps the child because it gives him the chance to compare his sentence directly with a sentence only slightly different in structure.

Most children will learn to speak with or without your conscious intervention, but how much pleasure they take in language and how well they are able to use language depends, to a large degree, on the adults around them.

Getting Ready to Read and Write

"Can I read my story to you?" five-year-old Benjie asked. He stood up from the table where he had been working for several minutes with markers and crayons. In his hand, he held sheets of construction paper folded into a "book."

Benjie climbed onto his mother's lap and intently "read" the story he'd written—about how his dog was lost and then found in the neighbor's yard. On the pages of his book, he had drawn pictures of the dog, himself, and several renditions of the letter *d*.

When Benjie finished, his mother gave him a big hug. Then she asked him why the dog had gone to the neighbor's yard. Benjie's face lit up. He scrambled off her lap and added a page with a picture of the dog chasing a ball.

By encouraging Benjie to express himself on paper, by listening to him read his story, and by asking supportive, thought-provoking questions, Benjie's mom conveyed to him the attitude that reading is interesting, fun, and relevant.

According to many of today's educators, this encouragement is the greatest contribution parents can make to their children's interest in, and enjoyment of, reading.

Ways to Make Reading Fun

Children are most likely to see something as enjoyable when it involves their active participation and draws upon their experience. How can parents make reading an active experience? By pointing out how written words are used in the environment and by encouraging their children to express themselves verbally and in writing.

Children develop reading skills at different rates, but the

love of sounds, words, and communication starts in infancy. Below are suggestions for ways in which parents can help their children learn to love reading. These activities will set the stage so that your children will learn to read joyfully *when they are ready.*

Read aloud. Recent studies suggest that children who are read to have a much easier time learning to read. It's important to make reading together an experience that is not restricted to any one time. Bedtime stories are great, but there's a lot to be gained from reading together at other times, too.

While bedtime stories are (ideally) followed by quiet and shut-eye, books read at other times can be followed by more lively conversations. Ask your child who his favorite character was or what he thinks happened after the story ended. Point out the names of the author and illustrator to give your child a sense that stories are created by people like himself.

Encourage your child to participate in reading the book—whether by pointing to particular pictures or filling in words that have become familiar after the umpteenth repetition.

It's generally best to read together during relaxed moments, but such moments can be few and far between in a household with young kids. So take advantage of the few quiet times that occur naturally—even if only for a few moments—during the day:

- Read to your child while you're in the kitchen waiting for the spaghetti water to boil.

- Take a book to the doctor's office to read with your child in the waiting room.

44

- Take a book along on other outings to read together during waits: at the grocery store, at the train station, the schoolyard, or anywhere else where you end up having to pass time.

And if your quiet time is interrupted, it need not mean the end of your reading. Have your child make a book-mark to use when a story is interrupted by a phone call or a sibling's cry.

Ask specific questions. It is a good idea to ask your child about things he has done and seen and to have him retell his experiences. While this may not seem directly related to reading, the process of organizing ideas and information that occurs when you converse *is* related.

It's important, however, that your questions be specific. If you ask, "What happened at school today?" it may be hard for a child to remember and formulate an answer. Questions like "Who did you sit next to at lunch?" "Which story did the teacher read?" and "Who fed the rabbit?" will probably get more detailed answers. Be sure to ask for opinions: "What did you think of that store?" or "Do the twins in your class like to play together? Why?" Asking these questions gives a child practice thinking in terms of who, what, when, and why—mainstays in the written world. And asking what happened next helps exercise the sequencing skills needed to follow a story.

Listen. Be sure to give your child time to complete his thoughts and sentences. Young children may ramble, but no matter how convoluted, the point they're making is important to them. It requires patience, but you'll learn more by paying attention—and your child will know and appreciate it.

Write with your child. Thank-you notes, birthday cards, and letters to Grandma are all opportunities for self-expression. Whether it's writing his name or just the first letter of his name, being on the creative side of reading helps a child understand the writing-reading relationship better. Feeling proud of himself as an author, thinking through what to say and how to say it, and putting the marks on paper all contribute to an appreciation of reading.

Encourage your child to draw. For children, drawing is a form of storytelling. Encourage your children to use different media—paint, crayons, markers—and to tell you about their pictures. Remember, though, that saying "What is it?" can put a child on the spot and make him think that he has to identify all the lines and shapes. The more open-ended "Do you want to tell me about the story?" gives him more leeway to describe, fabricate, elaborate, and imagine.

Let the child who is ready to read choose a story to read to you. When children begin to read, they begin in a very holistic way—recognizing the word *stop,* for instance, because they've seen it frequently on signs. Later they begin to notice patterns in written language. In doing this, they are using three main rules:

1. **Phonics.** Children begin to notice that words that begin with a certain letter *sound* a certain way. They also notice that there are sound patterns at the middle and end of words.
2. **Sentence Structure.** Children know what kind of word would fit in a certain place in a sentence. For example, if a child reads the sentence, *The book was on the* ____, he won't guess that the last word is *red.* He knows intuitively that it has to be a noun.

3. **Meaning.** A child knows that a word has to make sense in a certain spot. If he comes across the sentence, *The book was on the* _____, he won't guess that the noun is *tiger.* Instead, he'll look for a noun like *table* or *shelf.*

Making mistakes is a natural part of the learning process. Some mistakes let you know that a child is really thinking. For example, a child who reads aloud, "The man built a nice home," when the last word is actually "house," has used meaning, and probably phonics, to figure out the word.

Use your local library. In most places, children can get library cards as soon as they can write their names somewhat legibly. Librarians are happy to recommend age-appropriate books on topics of interest. Libraries frequently have story hours for young children and other activities for older ones. And why not take out a book for yourself at the same time and set a good example?

Show that you value reading. While it may be hard to find a quiet time to read while your child is awake, demonstrating that you like to read helps convey the message that reading is an enjoyable thing to do. Even grown-ups do it! Look at your book while your child is looking at his.

The Object Is to Have Fun

The activities described above are intended to be fun and engaging for your child, but they are only guidelines. Adapt them to suit your child's interests and skills. Try them out. See which activities *your* child responds to.

By sharing these activities with your children, you will be helping them see reading as an integral part of their lives. In this way, you will raise a child who both knows how to read and *likes* to read.

• •
Going for a Walk with a Prereader

Have you and your prereader looked at every storybook in the house so often that the pages fall apart at a touch? Are both of you looking for new ways to practice reading skills?

Almost everything a prereader does during the day can become a preparation for reading. Many familiar pastimes involve understanding symbols, following paths, and identifying objects, shapes, or colors. Here are a few simple ways to offer practice in prereading skills, as you and your child take a walk around the neighborhood:

Read shapes. Many geometric shapes, already well known to a prereader, take on new meaning when they are spotted in objects on a neighborhood walk. For example, on closer examination, a car is actually a conglomeration of circles, rectangles, squares, and trapezoids.

Read logos. Are there restaurants or stores near where you live that feature prominent trademarks or logos? Point out any such logos to your child when you take your walk. Later, at home, you can draw the different logos on a piece of paper and ask your child to identify them.

Read a tree. Bark patterns in trees can look like pictures. Are there faces or other recognizable patterns in any old gnarled trees in your neighborhood? The cracks and ruts in the bark's surface can also be used as maze paths to trace with a finger.

Read colors. As you walk along together, you can play

the guessing game "I see something . . . ," using colors as clues. You can also turn the game around by asking your child to pick out something that's red, yellow, blue, green, gray, orange, or brown.

Read letters and numbers. Your walk could turn into a hunting game, as together you try to spot the numerals *1* to *10* on buildings, street signs, or license plates. Children may enjoy hunting down the letters of the alphabet this way, too.

Read the sky. Cloud pictures are easy to spot on a clear day when the sky is filled with puffy cumulous forms. Scanning the sky for clouds that look like familiar objects is a game that changes every time the wind blows.

Read traffic signs and symbols. Once you have pointed out traffic signals and have explained the significance of the red, yellow, and green lights, you can watch a signal direct traffic for a while. Observing the lights at work will be a lesson in communicating with symbols.

You can also find arrows on traffic signs and those painted on the street and explain their functions. Observe them at work, as well.

If, after all of this outdoor prereading practice, you're still not ready to return to old, familiar books, why not put together your own neighborhood book? Your child can dictate sentences to you about the things both of you have seen. For illustrations, you can include pictures drawn by your child, napkins (with familiar logos), photos of neighborhood friends and places, and any other found or created objects.

• •

CHAPTER FIVE

• • • • • •

Math—More than Numbers

"The *big* little duck is the mommy," said Annie. "And the *little* duck is the baby." She had finished counting the toy animals in the barn she had constructed and had moved on to grouping them into families. Without realizing it, Annie was using math concepts in her play.

Young children start off liking math. Learning about patterns, sizes, shapes, amounts, and other relationships is as natural to young children as eating and speaking. If you look at the activities and games children gravitate to, you'll see how many of them are based on mathematical ideas. From musical chairs to dominoes, from "Where Is Thumbkin?" to fitting tops on pots, preschoolers are immersed in math.

Math is so fundamental that Jean Piaget, the psychologist who taught us to respect the special logic of young children, viewed mathematical relations as a focal point of children's understanding of the world. One of Piaget's major contributions was to help point out the value of a child's touching, holding, lifting, and otherwise handling real objects to learn about their properties. He also stressed that these experiences form the basis for the more abstract thinking children develop later. The work of Piaget and others has had an impact on how math is viewed and taught today.

What Is Math?

Increasingly, computational skills, such as adding and subtracting, are considered just one aspect of mathematics— useful but not all that important. While it is certainly practical to know how to add and subtract, the calculator has freed us to see these skills as relatively mechanical. Math is based on the physical world: It's less of a paper-and-pencil kind of activity than we sometimes think. It is hands-on experience with real objects, complete with their textures and weights, that familiarizes children with a wide range of math concepts. Even grown-up mathematicians use three-dimensional models and real-life comparisons in problem solving as a way to understand relationships.

Many of the ideas that underlie math are really quite simple. Below are some of the most basic concepts. Recognizing how much of our everyday lives involves these math basics can be an eye-opener.

Comparing. Comparisons can be made with any real objects. How are the objects the same? How are they different? Comparisons can also be made between objects of different sizes. Which book is wide? Which book is narrow? Is there more juice in Brian's glass and less in Tara's? Which two crayons are the same color?

Making comparisons is fundamental to understanding relationships in math. Equations $(2+2=4)$ and equivalences (the four small squares are equal in area to the one big square) are based on knowing when things are the same and when they are different.

Sorting. Grouping objects by similarities is also basic to an understanding of mathematics. Whether it's sorting blocks or socks or pebbles, kids need experience with actual objects to get the idea that things can be grouped.

Grouping is fundamental to understanding that 5 is 5 is 5 . . . whether it's five raisins or five cars or five children. Groups may have qualities in common with each other—for instance, each group has five things in it. Another feature of groups is that all group members have something in common. For example, kids can sort out all the green clothes in the hamper or all the bath toys that float.

Sequencing. Young children tend to think in terms of extremes—big and little, fat and skinny, short and tall. It takes time and experience for them to grasp that there can be gradations—short, medium, and tall. And concepts such as tall, taller, and tallest are even more sophisticated. Yet handling objects of different sizes and dimensions (blocks, for example) gives kids the chance to see that relationships often go step by step.

Sequences in time also help children understand math better. Days follow a certain pattern: First we have breakfast, then lunch, then dinner. Certain activities, too, proceed in a set sequence: Mom always adjusts the car mirror, then fastens her seatbelt, then turns on the engine, then puts on the radio. Before young children can learn to tell time, they need to grasp the basics: that yesterday came before today, that tomorrow is always in the future.

Correspondence. One-to-one correspondence is the matching of objects in one set with objects in another set. Experience with making things correspond helps kids understand number concepts better. Learning that one straw goes into each of the milk glasses or that two raisins go on top of each cookie helps children grasp the idea of correspondence.

This idea is well developed in the story "The Three Bears," in which there are *three* bowls of porridge, *three* chairs, and *three* beds—one for each of the three bears.

And it's clear that one bowl or chair or bed goes with each of the bears.

A child with a lot of experience handling objects will have an easier time understanding number groups, multiplication, and division years later when these subjects are introduced formally in school.

Part/whole relationships. A wheel is a part of a tricycle. The handlebars are another part. Children play with whole objects all the time, but they don't always think of the parts separately. It may not be until an object is broken or a child is constructing a toy or building with blocks that the idea that a whole is made up of parts truly takes form.

Another aspect of part/whole relationships hits home for children when they're faced with sharing. There are two people and one orange. There are four children and three slices of pizza left over. Certainly, understanding the relationship of parts to the whole is basic to an eventual understanding of fractions and percentages.

How Can Parents Help Prepare Their Children for Learning Math?

There are many ways parents can introduce their children to math concepts through everyday activities. Keep in mind that by encouraging your children to handle and group and count actual objects, you're helping them develop a real understanding of the principles that underlie the formulas and equations they will learn later.

Here are some ways to encourage math learning:

Cooking. Math abounds in the kitchen. Let your child be an apprentice chef, and you'll give her food for much math thought. Just working with such ideas as "more," "less," "some," "a few," and "none" exposes her to the idea that you can compare quantities. She'll also learn that expressions of amounts are often relative and that there are many words that can be used to describe quantities. For example, cooking can involve adding a little "more" flour to the board on which you're kneading the bread.

Following recipes also provides informal (and often delicious) exposure to different types of standard measures—for example, pouring half a cup of flour, counting three teaspoons of vanilla, or finding a pint of cream among the taller quarts of milk in the supermarket. Cooking requires timing, too: stirring the pudding for five minutes or coming back after an hour to see if the bread has risen.

Kids in the kitchen get a first-hand look at measuring time and an understanding of what can happen during a certain amount of time. Even the eating can be a math experience: "I want *more* spaghetti sauce and *less* spaghetti."

Setting the table. Did your older child just invite a friend to stay for lunch? Is the entire Ohio branch of the family coming for Thanksgiving dinner? If you need an extra pair of hands and want to involve your child in some learning at the same time, ask her to help set the table. She can count out the plates, make sure that there are enough chairs to go around, and even make place cards. All of this helps her learn about correspondence.

Construction. If your child doesn't look like a carpenter, look again. Making things out of paper, wood, and other materials is not only fun; it also introduces a child to lots of math basics as she works with cartons, straws, leaves, sticks, and other items to create three-dimensional constructions—bridges, spaceships, whatever. With adult supervision and help, she can make things out of wood, too. Making toy boats, doll furniture, and trucks helps her learn about part/whole relations and about the difference between perpendicular and parallel.

If you're not comfortable using a hammer and nails with your child, try glue—it holds wood pieces together pretty well. Projects can be completed in different phases, if your child is old enough to wait. Completing projects in phases can be a useful lesson in sequencing. And what better way to discover the properties of "three dimensional" than first to put together and then to paint each of the sides of a dollhouse or toy garage?

Block building. Is it the civic center? The new library? The Statue of Liberty? Many types of blocks and construction toys lend themselves to math learning.

In trying to make walls that are the same height, children also discover that two square pieces can be equal in size to one rectangular piece. Kids get a lot of experience comparing and a chance to see what happens when things are and aren't the same, too. As they become more sophisticated builders, they figure out how to make windows, doors, and ramps.

Kids work hard on these constructions. Letting the building stand a few days before you ask that she dismantle it will give your child a chance for more play and renovation—and will let her know that her latest architectural contribution is valued.

Sorting laundry. Give a prize to anyone who can find the mate to the blue sock with the brown design around the toe! Sorting clothes may seem a humdrum chore to you, but to your child it can be an adventure in matching and comparing. She can help you put all the shirts or underwear together. Or she can sort everything into adults' clothes and children's. And folding gives her experience with shapes and symmetry.

Puzzles. Which way does the piece fit? Puzzles are popular with children because they offer a challenging and usually rewarding chance to deal with matching shapes and directions. If you and your child work on puzzles together, you can discuss some techniques for solving them: for instance, looking at shape clues and color clues, matching details, and finding continuity in the picture. And don't be surprised if there are some puzzles your child is more adept at than you are. (The ability to do twelve-piece puzzles of farm animals seems to decline with age!)

Money. Money is one of those mysteries of the adult world that children find most intriguing. Let your child learn the names and values of different coins. You can compare values and even sequence the coins by their worth. Playing store and helping make actual purchases gives children a better understanding of how money is saved, spent, and exchanged for goods and services.

Body awareness. "I'm five years old, I weigh 42 pounds, and I'm 44 inches tall in my blue sneakers." Learning their vital statistics is fun for kids. Scales and growth charts give them a chance not only to learn more about themselves but also to learn how size and weight are measured and what these measurements mean. Children can measure their friends, dolls, and even their pets.

A good introduction to measurement, which helps kids really understand the underlying concepts, is to use nonstandard measures. How many of Jenny's steps does it take to get to the other side of the yard? How many of Andrew's steps? When Daddy gets on the seesaw, does it take two or three children to balance?

As we share activities like these with our children, we're also using the language of mathematics in an easy, informal way, which makes it an everyday part of our children's vocabularies. Children who are comfortable with math language and math concepts are likely to be among those who consider math a favorite subject.

CHAPTER SIX

······

Social Skills

Social development follows a distinct pattern. To ensure their survival, babies must think they're the center of the universe. As they get older, and if their needs for self-centeredness have been met, they become more aware of the existence and then the needs of others. But that takes a lot of time.

Children have a hard time understanding that Mommy has a headache or that baby brother does *not* want to play soccer. In time, it becomes easier for them to conceive of other people's viewpoints. They understand more about the jobs people have, how people are related to one another, and that different people have different personalities. They also have a better sense that people can come from different places and that there were people who lived in the past. Finding that they have a secure place in the larger world can help them achieve in other areas.

Building social skills begins with a child's ability to accept himself and his place within the smaller society and within his own family. As he learns to navigate outside his family, he builds on the skills learned at home.

The Importance of Play

By looking at what goes on during play, parents can learn much about their children. They will discover, for example, the emotional undertones that run through seemingly simple activities. They will also find a wealth of clues about their child's mental and social development—in the child's conception of rules, which changes as he gets older; in the strategies he evolves for winning; and in the complexity of his interaction within the games. Finally, understanding what games mean to children helps parents understand their own roles in those games.

What Games Offer

Children love games for many reasons. High among them is the fact that games give the child a safe way to deal with challenges, to try on different roles and ways of being. In "Mother, May I?" or "Red Light, Green Light," for instance, the child who is "It" gets to be the authority figure, the boss. The other players, for their part, may engage in stealthy mischief while the boss is not looking. In other games, the challenge may be a physical one ("How fast can I run?") or a mental one ("How can I jump my friend's checkers and win the game?").

Many people think that game playing starts when children are four or five, with traditional activities like "Tag" or "London Bridge." Actually, the game-playing experience starts much earlier, before a baby can even talk. It might start with that old standard "Peek-a-Boo." Though this game is a long way from contract bridge, on a primitive level, it shares many of the features of later games. It involves certain moves that are never altered and are repeated by the adult and child, along with certain permissible variations. ''Peek-a-Boo'' does not have the uncertain outcome of more advanced games—it turns out the same every time. Yet for the child, there *is* suspense until Mom's or Dad's familiar face reappears; then there is delight.

What's Winning?

Much of the fun in group activities of early childhood, such as ''Here We Go 'Round the Mulberry Bush'' or ''The Farmer in the Dell,'' lies in the fact that they involve singing and moving in unison. ''Winning'' is not part of these games; what's important is the sense of togetherness the games provide, along with the fact that they allow children to playact certain situations or themes with psychological appeal. For instance, young children love to act out order and chaos. As Brian and Shirley Sutton-Smith point out in their book *How to Play with Your Children,* a game like ''Ring Around the Rosy'' gives children a chance to play with precision and disorder: the disciplined circle and the sudden collapse onto the floor. Youngsters particularly delight in the sight of a member of the adult world sprawled on the floor.

There are some favorites of the under-six set that do involve an uncertain outcome or contest—''A Ticket a Tasket,'' ''Duck, Duck, Goose,'' and others. But young children play those games on their own terms, without a firm grasp of the supposed objectives. Take Mary Ann, age three-and-a-half. Her preschool class was playing ''Drop the Handkerchief'' and she was ''It.'' When she dropped the handkerchief behind Sammy, he didn't notice at first. Mary Ann stopped a few steps away and waited. Finally, Sammy woke up and gave chase. Mary Ann took off, but she was soon far ahead of Sammy. She slowed down. When she reached Sammy's spot in the circle, where she would be "safe" if she sat down, she kept on going. Like most children her age, Mary Ann's feeling seemed to be that there was no point in running unless you were being chased, and no great hurry to end the fun. The fun is in the chase!

Should you try to help your child understand the *point* of such games? You can try, but you will probably have little impact. The child will get the point when he is ready. In the meantime, he's having fun playing the game his way.

Young children aren't entirely indifferent to winning and losing. Winning simply has a different meaning for them than it does for older kids. "Musical Chairs" is a good example of this distinction. It is an adult-directed game but one that children greatly enjoy—up to the point at which someone fails to get a chair. This outcome causes the chairless child great distress. Consequently, many a host has ended up trying the game *without* removing a chair. The young players are as excited as ever in their scramble for seats! The preschool child likes to win, yes, but there need not be any losers in order for him to feel like a winner.

It isn't until they're seven or eight that children truly pay attention to the action of their playmates and to the existence of common rules. And now, for the first time, the child sees winning as determined by what he has done *in relation to* what the other players have done. Now hitting ten home runs isn't winning if your opponent's team hits eleven. "Musical Chairs" isn't fun unless there's the risk of not getting a chair. The pleasures of games were previously individual, though the child liked having others around. Now games are truly social, with fixed rules.

Although children of seven or eight can play games with common rules, they still have a relatively primitive concept of what a rule is. For them, rules are eternal, God-given, parent-given. Throughout childhood, the concept of rules evolves until finally, older children see rules as based on common consent and subject to change by mutual agreement.

The Parent's Role

Parents can contribute to their youngsters' enjoyment of games by creating an atmosphere of playfulness and fun. There are also some specific things that every parent can do to enhance a child's development through play.

- **Watch your child for clues.** By noticing the aspects of games that catch and hold a child's interest and the strategies he uses, parents can improve their sense of what and how to play with him.

  They may wish, for instance, to simplify a game or to add a new variation. They will learn when a game is likely to get too frustrating for the child and what methods they can use to offset differences in skill without diminishing his pleasure in the game. Noting what aspects he can handle, parents also get a sense of when it may be fruitful to explain a rule or strategy and when, because of the child's developmental level, it may be pointless.

- **Know when you shouldn't get involved.** Learning when *not* to play is important for parents, too. Don't play when you're too preoccupied, too grouchy, or too tired to enjoy yourself. Children pick up on those feelings— and the pleasure goes out of the game for both you and them.

- **Don't rush in to smooth things over when children disagree.** With peers, children argue, compromise, compete, and work out their ideas of fairness in ways they cannot with adults. They should be left to learn in their way.

- **Don't interfere when your child is losing a game.** You may feel your advice will help, but your child will lose the practice needed to sharpen problem-solving skills. At the same time, the other players may think your assistance is unfair, and your child won't enjoy an empty victory. (See sidebar below for tips on teaching your child problem-solving strategies.)

Parents initiate young children into the ways of games. At later ages, although it is still fun to share family games, the parent is less heavily involved. Whatever the child's age, it's important for parents to be aware of how productive games are for their children's growth. When parents understand the developmental function of games, it's easier to stand back and give children room. One of the best gifts you can give your child is the time and freedom to play.

• •

It's How You Play the Game: Helping Your Child Develop Problem-Solving Strategies

When six-year-old Eddie begins to have trouble with the puzzle he's working on, he pushes the pieces aside and quits. "Oh, I don't have a good enough memory," he says. "I'll never figure this out!"

Brian has a different reaction. "Well, I guess I'd better try harder. But I'll figure it out any second now."

Why does one child throw up his hands at the first sign of frustration, while another child meets all obstacles head-on?

"How children deal with success and failure is not related to how smart they are," says Dr. Carol Dweck, a psychologist at the University of Illinois who has done research on this topic. "It's not related to their abilities at all but to how they interpret their successes and, particularly, their failures."

Two Approaches to Problems

Different children react in different ways to frustration, Dr. Dweck's research showed. Some children may make mistakes, but they keep on trying and eventually figure out what has to be done. Others give up rather quickly if they can't find a solution. The difference is in the way the children view their failure to solve the problem immediately.

"Children who persist don't take their setbacks personally," she explains. "These children are unfailingly positive and actually seem to get happier at the challenge. They become intense and excited and try new strategies."

On the other hand, children who give up quickly are the ones who blame their initial failure on a lack of ability—even though they are very capable and may have performed the same task successfully at another time. "These children think they're not as good as they want to be, and they very quickly start to berate themselves," Dr. Dweck points out.

These children are also very concerned with their image. They worry about how competent they look to others, about competing with children who might appear better than they. "When you're so concerned that you're going to look and feel incompetent if you lose, then you have a lot at stake each time you compete," says Dr. Dweck.

The desire to achieve is not bad in itself, she goes on, but it is a problem when a child sees it as defining his or her worth.

How Parents Can Help

Parents can do a number of things that will help their children grow up willing to accept challenges, Dr. Dweck says. Here are a few:

- **Don't criticize the child's failure. Offer suggestions instead.** Instead of delivering a personal condemnation of a child's personality or ability, an adult could offer the child help in learning to overcome failure. If a child loses a game he is playing with a parent, for example, the parent might suggest, "Maybe you just have to try harder next time. How can you change your strategy?" The child's abilities should not be an issue.

- **Don't purposely let your child win.** "If you know your child gets upset when he loses, you'll probably think you should let the child win to build up his confidence," Dr. Dweck says. "But that backfires. Research has found that that kind of unbroken success has made children *more* sensitive to failure when it does occur."

- **In general, don't give rewards.** "When there are external rewards, children may lose their internal motivation to perform," Dr. Dweck explains. Children who overcome failures do so because they want to achieve a personal mastery. Offering children rewards for achievement takes the focus away from pleasure in the achievement itself. She adds, however, that if a child is doing very poorly or has behavior problems, external inducements can be helpful. "But the emphasis should be on phasing them out."

The idea, then, is to ease the pressures to achieve that children might feel. "Parents can help their children feel that it's not necessary to be better than everyone all the time," says Dr.

Dweck. "We want children to learn not to worry what others are going to think of them and not to think that setbacks mean they're incompetent."

These kinds of messages, she says, will help children develop the confidence they need to meet life's challenges.

• •
The Shy Child

Many children who play contentedly on their own much of the day are not shy; they are simply introverted. By inclination, they engage in a lot of solitary activity or play quietly alongside another child or two, but they are quite comfortable and engaged. Shy children, on the other hand, are anxious and tense; they would like to join in but can't.

As the parent of a shy child, you can take the following actions to keep shyness from becoming a problem:

- **Give your child a range of social experiences from infancy on.** As Dr. Philip Zimbardo and Dr. Shirley Radl write in *The Shy Child: A Parent's Guide to Preventing and Overcoming Shyness from Infancy to Adulthood,* "Sheer lack of experience in social settings contributes to shyness." If a child has had little contact with other children, he has had little opportunity to develop the social skills that will allow him to "mix and mingle," and therefore he may naturally be intimidated when thrust into their midst.

- **Take things gradually.** Social situations that overwhelm a child contribute to shyness, especially when the child is naturally slow to warm up. Dropping your three-year-old off at a birthday party where he knows only one or two children or asking your reticent daughter to sing for a roomful of adults may be providing them with "social experiences," but it isn't providing social comfort. For the most part, the sink-or-swim approach is likely to produce more sinking than swimming.

- **Give your child experiences with playmates and play situations that are nonthreatening.** All children, shy children especially, should have opportunities to play with children who do not dominate or intimidate them. Having your shy child play with a younger child is often a good way to build up your child's confidence and social skills and to give him more positive feelings about social interaction.

  Allowing him to play on his home turf with another child can also reassure him. In addition, you can help your child learn games in advance so he may be more likely to join in when the opportunity is there.

- **Do not label your child "shy" or allow anyone else to do so.** When parents are embarrassed by a child's unwillingness to greet or respond to a visitor, they may say, "He's a little shy." Such remarks can be harmful. The child begins to think of himself as shy, even if he hasn't thought so before.

- **Build your child's self-esteem and competence.** Experts agree that low self-esteem is a major source of shyness. Shy people tend to expect a lot of themselves and continually worry that they are inadequate. Your affectionate support and honest compliments are especially important for your child. Replace his negative statements about himself with positive and constructive action. Suppose your child says, "None of the kids like me." Restrain the instinct to vent your anger at the children ("Well they aren't half as smart as you, anyway" or "Don't pay any attention to them. What do they know?"). This attitude just adds to the child's feelings of being an outsider. Instead say, "They'll like you when they know you better. Now, let's think of some things we could do to help you and your friends get to know each other."

• •

A Word About Manners

On one level, manners are lists of rules: *Don't litter. Use your napkin to wipe your face. Don't interrupt when others are talking.* Thinking of manners in this way can be pretty confusing for adults as well as for children. For one thing, many of the rules are changing. Should your child call your adult friend *Sir, Mr. Smith,* or *Dan?* You have to decide without help from the authorities.

Fortunately, manners are more than a set of commandments about which fork to use. "Following the rules isn't the same as being considerate," says Sara Gorfinkle, of Manners House Calls, a New York City agency that instructs children in polite behavior. "Knowing the rules doesn't mean the child has generosity of spirit." If you want your child to be truly courteous, you need to cultivate his respect for the feelings and needs of others.

Of course, children are notoriously egocentric, so even simple niceties, such as waiting their turn in conversation, go against the grain. On the other hand, children also show an early awareness of the feelings of others. "Even before the age of two, children will become silent and very concerned when another child is unhappy," says Dr. Laura Dittman, professor emeritus in child development at the University of Maryland. "That concern for other people's feelings is the substratum of manners." Parents can strengthen it by helping children recognize other people's feelings and motivations. ("See, the girl is sad because her block tower fell down," or "Aunt Martha must have looked hard to pick out that present.")

Although manners seem to be primarily for the benefit of others, they also have hidden rewards for children. Research shows that children who know what's expected of them have higher self-esteem than those whose parents have few rules. "Living up to expectations confirms that you've done a good job," notes Dr. Don Hamachek, professor of psychiatry at Michigan State University.

Knowing how to behave properly also gives children social confidence. For instance, the shy child who hides behind his mother's skirt when introduced to a stranger may simply not know what to say. If he's given his part of the dialogue ("How do you do? I'm glad to meet you"), he may be able to handle the situation with more assurance.

Children also thrive on the positive feedback from adults that good manners bring them.

When should parents start teaching manners? "Magic" words such as "please," "thank you," and "excuse me" are easily acquired during the second year, when children are just learning to speak. Once they can say the words, children may need prompting to use them in the right places, but parents shouldn't be too quick with reminders. "Sometimes parents don't give children time to say these things," Dittman points out. "They rush in and provide the right answer out of anxiety about having the child look good."

The truth is that kids between two and five won't "look good" much of the time. According to Hamachek, "Kids under five tend to be free-spirited. They don't know all the rules of the game and tend to do things on impulse." He believes parents should talk to young children about social rules and point them out without expecting their children to follow them all the time.

That's a difficult role for parents. After you've told your child to chew with his mouth closed for the twentieth time, you may feel as though he's deliberately disobeying you. Actually, he's just having the inevitable trouble we all have changing an old habit. "Kids need to be reminded," says Hamachek. "That doesn't mean the kids are rude or the parents are bad. Becoming well-mannered isn't something that happens in a week. If parents understood that, they might not get so frustrated and angry."

If anything, parents need to mind their own manners when correcting their children. "Don't overrespond when the rules are broken," advises Hamacheck. Gorfinkle agrees: "Parents who punish too soon and too severely may make a child passive and shy for fear of saying the wrong thing at the wrong time. The rules should be repeated nicely and kindly. The child should never feel humiliated."

Often parents overreact because they feel exposed when a child behaves poorly in public. "Parents often feel they are being judged by the behavior of their child and are found wanting," says Dittman. "Their own self-esteem is threatened."

In these situations, it's helpful to remember two things: First, yours is not the first, last, or only child to have stood whining at your elbow while you were trying to talk to another adult. As Hamachek notes, "Lots of parents have the feeling that 'only my child is like this,' but all kids are like that."

The second thing to remember is that you are a separate person from your child. Though you certainly influence his behavior, you don't control it. So when your child misbehaves in public, try to separate your own feelings of being betrayed ("How could you?") from the need to correct your child.

Sometimes you can sidestep public problems by realistically assessing your child's social skills before you go out. A child who still screams when he wants milk may not yet be ready to eat in a restaurant. A child who has stopped screaming but still eats with his fingers might be more comfortable and behave more appropriately in a fast-food restaurant than a fancy one. A child who can manage a fork and sit for half an hour might try quick-serve diner meals before working up to three courses in a fancy restaurant. Putting your child into a situation that he can't yet handle reveals your bad manners—not his.

With older children who have had more experience, be clear about your expectations in advance. Simply saying, "Behave yourself" doesn't provide much information about what you want the child to do. Instead, be precise and positive: "Please use your fork and keep your voice down in the restaurant."

Be equally clear about consequences: "If you make too much noise, we'll have to leave." Then follow through, without anger, if possible. "There's a big difference between picking a child up to go and yanking him out of his chair," says Hamachek. "If the parent stays calm, the child learns not only that there are rules but also that adults can be angry without throwing things."

The other way to avoid public problems is to practice good manners at home. According to Gorfinkle, meals are an obvious opportunity: "I tell parents of my students that the best way to reinforce what their children have learned is to have dinner with them at least three nights a week. Mealtime is the most important time of day. A child can socialize, share ideas, learn patience, and practice table manners."

For this to work, you have to be casual and low-key about correcting your child. If your child is eating with his fingers, say simply, "It's more polite to use your fork." Don't nag and don't get into a power struggle. Just mention the rule and let it go. "Kids want to please adults in their lives," says Hamachek. But they are most likely to do this when they feel as though it's their choice and not a parent's demand.

Practical Approaches

Here are some other pointers on raising courteous kids:

- **Set a good example.** Says Gorfinkle: "There's no point in trying to teach children manners if they aren't exhibited between parents. If there's courtesy between husband and wife, children grow up hearing 'May I?' and 'Thank you.'" It's also important to be polite to your child. Although parents are within their rights to say, "Pick up your toys," adding a "please" not only gets the message across but gives a lesson in courtesy.

- **Explain the "why" behind the rule.** "Everything has a reason," says Gorfinkle, "and I try to explain it." For example, during classes Gorfinkle will slouch down in the chair and ask the children what she looks like. They will usually say things like, "You don't want to be here" or "You don't want to talk to us," giving her the opportunity to explain why sitting in a certain way is inappropriate.

- **Give your child a role in social events whenever possible.** "If company is coming, you can provide a plan," advises Dittman. "Perhaps your child can pass the cookies or the hors d'oeuvres." If he's not a bored bystander, he's less likely to become intrusive and demanding.

- **If you have to correct a child, do it discreetly.** Children are very sensitive to what others think of them, and a public reprimand of your child may embarrass him so much that he'll act worse than before. This is particularly important if your child has made an amusing mistake. "Children want to learn how to do things right," says Dittman, "and they shouldn't be permitted to feel foolish."

- **Don't let manners override your child's feelings.** For instance, if someone gives your child a toy for his birthday that he already owns, you may teach him to say "Thank you" without mentioning the duplication. Then, once you're in private, acknowledge his disappointment. "It's important to validate a child's feeling," Dittman says. "You don't want children to hide or deny their feelings just for the sake of manners."

- **Focus on one or two areas at a time.** If you're working on telephone manners, loosen up at mealtime. Children are learning self-control, but they can't exert it all the time. A child who is trying hard to share when a friend comes to visit may find an excuse to throw a tantrum when the friend leaves.

- **Try to understand a breach of manners from your child's point of view.** For example, interrupting when you're on the phone may seem like simple discourtesy to you, but it may be something quite different for your child. As Dittman points out, "Your child may feel anxious because he's shut out of your attention, so he may try wildly to get you back." If you understand the source of your child's misbehavior, you may be able to help him cope in this instance by letting him sit on your lap while you talk.

Learning manners is a gradual process to be sure. But helping children acquire social skills that allow them to deal with the larger world is essential.

Integrating the Disabled Child into the Social Mainstream

Two five-year-olds enter the playground, each with a mother in tow. One child runs toward the other, stops abruptly when he notices the other child's crutches, turns to his mother, and asks, "What's wrong with *her*, Mommy?"

If this scene involved your child, how would you respond? The answer you choose may depend upon whether your child is the one asking the question or the one who has a disability. In either case, you've just been presented with an opportunity to help your child develop a positive attitude toward people who are different from him.

There has never been a better time for our children to grow with an understanding of disabilities. More and more children with all types of physical, mental, and emotional disabilities are now attending school and participating in community activities alongside their nondisabled peers. Both disabled and nondisabled children today have opportunities to share meaningful experiences and simply to get to know one another. With the help and encouragement of the adults around them, *all* children can learn acceptance and mutual appreciation. But just how do we encourage this acceptance?

First of all, we need to examine our own feelings because our children take their cues from us. If we respond to questions about disabilities with embarrassment, our children will learn that a disability somehow connotes shame. If, on the other hand, we respond in a way that emphasizes the individuality of the disabled person—and not the disability of the individual—we will have paved the way for greater understanding among all children.

Respond to Curiosity

All children are curious about the people around them and are likely to ask questions about things they don't understand. If your child is not disabled and does not know people with disabilities, the first such encounter will probably trigger a series of questions. "What's wrong with her?" may be the only question he asks, but he may really be wondering, "Is the disability a punishment for something?" or, "Can I catch it?" At this point, it is important to remember that it is lack of knowledge, not lack of sensitivity, that brings on the questions. By providing the knowledge, we can instill the sensitivity we want in our children. The following are some ways to foster an understanding of disabilities in nondisabled children:

- **When questions arise about a disabled person, don't scold your child for his curiosity.** Instead, tell him, in terms he can understand, what you know about the nature of the disability, but do it in a way that will not offend the disabled person. Reassure your child that the disabled person is in no way responsible for his or her disability and that the condition is not something that will happen to your child.

- **Don't wait for your child to verbalize his questions,** because doubts and fears that are permitted to persist inevitably lead to intolerance in later years. So if you notice your child reacting uncomfortably to a disabled person, discuss his reaction. In so doing, be sure to discuss the person's abilities along with his or her disabilities.

- **In all discussions about disabilities, accurately depict the extent of the disability.** For instance, help your child to understand that a blind person is not helpless; he just can't see. A deaf person is different from a hearing person only in that he cannot hear. And a person with Down syndrome is able to learn; it just takes more time.

Use the Neighborhood As a Resource

Even before your child indicates that he wants to learn about disabilities, you can set the stage for positive learning experiences by using the community as an "open classroom." You might begin by asking him to tell you about children with special needs in his school or play group. Talk about people you know with disabilities and share experiences and reactions that *you* had as a child. In addition, you can plan activities that will add to your child's understanding. For instance:

- **On everyday excursions, discuss the purpose of wheelchair ramps, telephone booths, and bathroom facilities designed to be accessible to people in wheelchairs.** At home, when watching television, discuss the "closed-captioned" symbol that precedes certain broadcasts.

- **Plan special excursions, such as a trip to a training school for seeing-eye dogs, a wheelchair basketball game, a Special Olympics meet, or a performance by a deaf theater company.** Also plan a visit to the Braille and large-print book section of the library and to the telephone store for a demonstration of phones that have been designed for hearing-impaired customers.

- **When visiting the library or planning your television viewing, seek out books and shows that depict the disabled as contributing members of society.** Plan on reading and viewing along with your child so that questions can be answered and discussions can be encouraged.

- **Encourage your child's school to invite guest speakers on disabilities,** to show films that explain both the abilities and the disabilities of disabled persons, and to plan activities that involve both special-needs classes and regular classes.

Extend Concepts at Home

Teaching positive attitudes in a conscious way is one means of raising considerate children. But it's by example, more than by words, that we are likely to make a lasting impression. When encountering a disabled store clerk who may take a long time to count out your change, be patient. Don't park in spaces that are reserved for disabled drivers, even if you're "only stopping for a minute." Avoid using expressions such as "That's retarded!" in everyday speech. Creating an atmosphere of respect for others will help a child interact with his disabled peers. The following are some ways to foster that interaction:

- **Teach your child how to begin a conversation with a child or adult who is disabled.** For example, after the initial "Hello," suggest that the child make an observation such as "I like your hat," or ask a question such as "Do you live around here?" Such a conversation will lead the child closer to an understanding of the person to whom he is speaking and helps to put the disability in perspective—as just an aspect of the disabled person's whole self.

- **When choosing toys for your child, consider dolls that show a child with a disability.** The message is that it's okay to be different.

- **Plan experimental games so that your child can begin to understand how it feels to have a disability.** Using a blindfold can help make a sighted child aware of the needs of the blind. Turning off the volume on the television can give a child some understanding of deafness. Trying to reach a usually accessible light switch from a seated position can help a child see the world from the point of view of someone in a wheelchair. Use your judgment to decide whether your child is mature enough to handle and benefit from these games. And remember that the reason behind any of these experiences is to sensitize children, not to point out "how lucky they are" that they do not share the disability. Such a point of view could reinforce the mistaken concept that the disabled are somehow responsible for their disabilities.

- **Along with your child, learn the sign language for some simple phrases,** since many people with a variety of disabilities use a total-communication method based on sign language.

- **Most important, encourage your child to find friendship among a wide variety of people—those with and without disabilities.** Help him overcome any inhibitions he may have by inviting disabled classmates and neighborhood children for an afternoon play date, birthday party, or family outing. Consider broadening your own circle of friends to include the disabled.

As parents, we *can* make a difference in the attitudes our children develop about themselves and about those around them. Along with our children, we can learn that people with disabilities are individuals who have a variety of interests and talents. We are the ones who "handicap" people by labeling them—or by simply overlooking them. And we are the ones who can replace fear and misunderstanding with a deep appreciation for all of our children.

Helping the Disabled Child

For all children, growing up involves learning to appreciate their unique gifts and learning to accept their limitations. For disabled children, the growing-up process will be more complicated. Their siblings, too, will have to make special adjustments. And their parents will face challenges not encountered by parents of nondisabled children. If you are the parent of a disabled child, what can you do to enhance your child's self-esteem?

Your first responsibility is to help him know that he is loved and appreciated just for himself. Beyond that, here are some specific steps you can take to ensure that he grows up with an acceptance of himself:

- **Explain the nature of his disability or condition to him, and don't be afraid to talk about your child with family, friends, and neighbors.** The result may be that they will become more accepting and comfortable with your child and thus help him to be more comfortable with himself.

- **Give your child the opportunity to talk about his feelings,** fears, and frustrations, his anger about having a disability, and his difficulties in dealing with everyday life. Don't be his only sounding board, however, because there may be things he'd rather not discuss with you. Make sure that he has access to counselors and to other children and adults with similar disabilities.

- **Structure play experiences with nondisabled children of a comparable age.** You need to allow your child to take risks, despite the stress it may cause. Help prepare him for interaction with other children by helping him develop a repertoire of interests typical of children his age, such as playing interactive games, going to the movies, listening to music, and participating in sports. By encouraging the skills and aptitudes that your child does have, you can enable him to participate competitively with nondisabled peers.

- **Follow the same techniques used with nondisabled children to foster compassion,** because sometimes a child who has been a victim of others' cruelty may, in turn, be unkind to a child more vulnerable than himself.

- **Erase the word** *can't* **from your vocabulary, and refrain from the temptation of limiting your expectations for your child.** All children have a way of surprising us with what they can do.

- **Be informed.** Know your child's rights, and don't be afraid to be his advocate in school and elsewhere in the community. Know which community resources exist, and where programs don't exist, demand them. Help your community be informed, too. Consider writing a newspaper article about the rights of the disabled or speaking before the local PTA or other civic organizations.

What About Siblings?

Children in any family need to learn to adjust to the needs of their siblings, but for children whose siblings are disabled, the adjustment process is somewhat different. Younger brothers and sisters of a child with disabilities learn acceptance of a disabled sibling as part of life. They are almost intuitively aware of differences, but they still need explanations and open discussions about their sibling's disability.

Siblings who experience the birth of a sister or brother with special needs or those who must confront the unexpected disability of a sibling will—like you—need time to adjust. And as they adjust, they will experience emotions unique to the siblings of a disabled child. For example, at times they may sense your strain and may feel that they have to be on good behavior all the time—an impossible task. Or they may perceive that their brother or sister is receiving a greater share of your time and attention and will feel resentful. They may also resent the fact that they occasionally have to take care of a sibling, often restricting their own activities. Along with this resentment, there usually will be guilt. They may feel guilty, too, simply because they are "normal."

Perhaps the greatest stress on siblings is dealing with social situations. There may be times when your child feels shame or embarrassment. He may be the target of teasing or insensitivity by other children. He may temporarily avoid being seen with his disabled sister or brother. And as the sibling of a disabled child grows older, he may also be concerned that in the future he will have to shoulder the burden of responsibility for his sister or brother. More than most, he may have fears that someday he, too, will have a child who is disabled.

Address Their Concerns

As a parent you need to give a concise, direct, and honest explanation of the nature and extent of a brother's or sister's disability. Your conversation should not only answer the "how" and "why" of the disability but should also address the natural concerns about how his or her own life will likely be affected.

Your nondisabled child knows or will soon discover the many pluses of having a brother or sister with a disability. Most brothers and sisters gain immeasurably from the pride they share in the accomplishments, successes, and achievements of their disabled sibling. What they need help with is learning to cope with their own emotions and the social pressures outside of your home. As a parent, you can help foster the positive aspects of your children's relationship in a number of ways. For example:

- **Be sure there are opportunities for your nondisabled child to discuss his feelings with others,** such as a counselor, another impartial adult, and other children who have a brother or sister with a disability.

- **When talking with your nondisabled child refrain from using the expression "special child" when referring to your child with a disability.** After all, every child needs to know that he is special to his parents.

- **The most important thing to remember is that, like any siblings, disabled and nondisabled children alike need to be recognized and understood as unique individuals.**

All children, as they grow older, come to realize that we can't always be there for them, that we can't always alleviate their hurts, and that we can't always make miracles. But if we teach our children—those with and without disabilities—to accept and love themselves, we will have given them the foundation to grow into the best people they can be.

The Importance of Developing a Sense of Humor

From an infant's first giggle to an adult's appreciation of subtle wit, a person's ability to laugh, to make others laugh, and to see the humor in everyday situations is more than a pleasant diversion from the serious side of life. Recent studies have shown that a sense of humor promotes good emotional and physical health. A sense of humor also enhances communication by developing language skills and by diffusing the negative emotions that can interrupt productive conversation. Even without adult prompting, a child is at work defining and refining this life skill. When adults willingly join in the fun, however, the child's talent for laughter grows.

How do children know what's funny? It depends largely on the age and verbal abilities of each child and on that child's ability to pick up clues that something is meant to be funny.

A two-year-old, for instance, will laugh at the sight of an older brother putting a glove on his head. His response reflects his knowledge of the world around him: He knows the difference between hats and gloves, and he can recognize that his brother is upsetting the natural order of things.

Like most two-year-olds, he can take delight in comfortable surprises—the jack-in-the-box that pops up at the right moment, the ball that plops into the water fountain with a big splash, the silly picture book of a dog on roller skates. A year ago, however, the jack-in-the-box frightened him, the splashing ball made him cry, and the dog on roller skates seemed perfectly normal. He didn't yet know enough about the world to laugh at a glove on his brother's head.

As his language abilities increase, so will his repertoire of jokes. By age three he will discover that calling a known object by another name can be very funny—both to himself and to any other three-year-olds in the room. "This is my hat," he may say while putting on his mittens. Or he might make up a new word for "hat" and announce, "I'm putting my 'gukky' on my head now." Children learning how to play with language often mislabel to an extreme, describing people and objects in opposite terms. For instance, he will call his hulking father "my little daddy" or his small stuffed teddy bear "my big dinosaur." These playful misnamings are a way for young children to show that they have already grasped the basics of language and that they are so comfortable with object names that they can risk letting go of them for a while.

Proof of competence is the basis for another common theme in the jokes of preschoolers: the toilet. Though most parents find it difficult to appreciate a joke whose punchline is a variation of the phrase "nanny-nanny poo-poo," four- and five-year-olds usually can't resist bathroom humor.

There are two reasons why young children find bathroom jokes so funny. These jokes present a way of dealing with some of the tension young children associate with learning how to use the toilet. Telling a joke about it is a way of announcing to their peers that they have, indeed, mastered the art. Laughing at a friend's bathroom joke is the nonverbal equivalent of saying, "Yeah, me too." The other reason why young children find these jokes appealing is that they are just beginning to sort words into "good words" and "bad words." (Up until this point, any word they learned was "good" simply because they were able to learn it.) When they find that taboo words can trigger a reaction in adults, they feel an unaccustomed level of control. It becomes fun and exciting to use words in this new way and to demonstrate the power that their evolving language skills has given them.

On to Punchlines

"What has four wheels and flies?" If you answered, "A garbage truck," you probably live with a six- or seven-year-old who has reached a level of comfort with his ability to recognize that a single word can have more than one meaning. Children in the early school years become intrigued, sometimes obsessed, with riddles, puns, and other structured jokes. It takes a lot of skill to tell these jokes, since each one has to be told just so or it loses its meaning. A younger sibling who was able to recognize the joke format might be unable to understand the punchline. The answer seems absurd and therefore, he decides that for a punchline to work, it must make no sense. A preschooler, for example, could mimic the above joke by asking, "What has four wheels and flies?" His punchline, "My umbrella!," will be very funny to him. For children his age, simply recognizing the "setup" and expecting something to be funny is reason enough to laugh. Understanding the word play behind the punchline will come later.

The kind of spontaneous joking and comfortable bantering that are mainstays of adult conversation begin to emerge at the age of six or seven, when children are beginning to become more social. For youngsters this age, telling jokes and riddles is often a preferred way of communicating. Since riddles and ''Knock-knock'' jokes guarantee some sort of response, they make great conversation starters. Children collect and exchange jokes and are always trying to stump one another—and you—with a ''good one.'' In group situations, six- and seven-year-olds are beginning to learn that laughter can ease tension and diffuse competition.

How Can Parents Help Bring Out the Humor in Their Children?

They can begin by making humor part of their child's life:

- **Kid around with your kid.** Children love it. You'll love it. Laughing and joking and being just plain silly are some of the best things about being a child—or a parent. Whether it's tickling or making funny faces at each other or retelling old, familiar jokes, your child will get the message that it's fun to have fun.

- **Discover what makes your child laugh and join him at his level.** Follow your child's cues. If he's making up a silly rhyming poem, for example, join in with your own silly verse.

- **Expose your child to your own, more grown-up, sense of humor.** If something strikes you as funny, tell him why you're laughing.

- **Expose your child to different types of humor.** From the slapstick comedy of Laurel and Hardy to the subtle wit of Mary Poppins, there's a lot of funny material just waiting to be discovered by your child. Much of the best can be enjoyed by adults as well. Consider watching old

Charlie Chaplin films or reruns of the "Our Gang" comedies on TV. Read Sunday comics together with your child.

- **Encourage your child's expression of humor.** Young children's jokes can be so silly that even the most doting parents may want to roll their eyes and say, "Give me a break." But parents who encourage the young comedian might eventually have the last laugh. Listen to your child's jokes and try to act amused. It will help him maintain a comic spirit that will lead him toward newer and funnier material. Help him make up his own variations of jokes he hears. You can also encourage your child's gift for comedy by writing down his jokes. Even the ones you don't find funny now will give you all a good laugh years from now as you reread these early attempts.

- **Use humor to diffuse potentially stressful situations.** You're late for work, your child won't put on his shoes, and the tension is building. You could yell, but neither of you would feel much better. Or you could suggest that bare feet are too easy to tickle as you playfully help him finish getting dressed. Or try a verbal joke: On a hot summer day, say, "We'll need our shoes to get to the North Pole today."

Social skills, as we've seen, involve all the many advanced interactions your child will experience as he moves from playing peek-a-boo with you to having a job interview years from now. More than academic skills, the ability to get along with others will serve a child well as he finds his place in the world.

CHAPTER SEVEN

· · · · · ·

Science—Early Explorations

Look!'' said Lisa as she watched the ladybug crawl across the leaf. ''That ladybug has two dots on her back.''

''Can she fly?'' asked her friend Joey, looking up from digging for worms nearby.

''I don't know,'' Lisa answered. She bent down and looked closely. ''Maybe. She kind of has wings.''

Just then, as if on cue, the ladybug fluttered over to another clump of leaves. ''She *can* fly, she *can*,'' shouted Joey with that combination of wonder and excitement special to children under six.

Young children are natural scientists. Intuitively, they do many of the same things that grown-ups wearing lab coats do. For professional and child alike, science is the process of finding out more about how the world works. Both observe, predict, and form conclusions based on what they see. And much of science takes place outside the laboratory—scientists do some very productive thinking while brushing their teeth, feeding the cat, and listening to rain on the roof. For children, day-to-day life offers infinite opportunities to watch, explore, probe, and discover more about the world, too.

There are a number of ways parents can encourage and develop the scientific thinking children display so naturally. One of the most essential is to recognize that ''science'' can occur anywhere: in the kitchen, in the backyard, or in the bathtub. Another is to understand that you don't have to be a "scientist" to foster your child's normal curiosity. Young children don't need to be bombarded with facts. While seven- and eight-year-olds love to spout bits of information, younger kids are more interested in—and attuned to—the *process* of science. If you explore alongside your child, you will help her retain her natural enthusiasm for learning how things work and develop some science skills at the same time.

Scientific Thinking

To encourage scientific thinking, there are specific skills you can develop with your child:

- **Observing.** This perfectly ordinary activity is at the very core of science. Noticing how things look and how they feel, taste, smell, and sound is fundamental to learning about the world. There are a variety of ways to use your senses, and you can share these with your child. For instance, you and your child can close your eyes and just listen to the sounds around you.

- **Describing experiences.** Encourage kids to talk about what they see, hear, taste, smell, and touch. You might get responses like: "This leaf has jaggedy edges and this one has smooth edges." "The sky is cloudy and the ground is dark." "Sour juice makes my tongue feel tickly."

    Children use very colorful descriptive language that often captures their perceptions in unique ways. Ask questions that bring out these imaginative descriptions. Also, help them find appropriate words when they need them—words such as *sour, sticky, lumpy, shiny, crackly, or crisp.*

If your child says, "The bench feels cold when I touch it," you might suggest she find out if the jungle gym and seesaw handle also feel cold, "since they're all made of metal."

Or, "I knew Daddy was coming up the stairs." "How?" "Because of the sound of the footsteps—they were loud and slow. Aunt Jane's are fast."

Children can describe their experiences in many ways—not just verbally. Encourage them to use drawing, writing, pantomime, mimicking sound, or singing to translate what they observe through their senses.

- **Finding similarities and differences.** Another way to sharpen observation is to suggest that children look closely for the ways things are alike and different. How are all the people on the beach the same? "Everyone's barefoot except Sean, who's wearing sandals." "Two of the birds seem to like what's in the birdfeeder, but the other one just wants to play."

- **Collecting.** Young children love to collect and sort things into categories. Yours may want to acquire leaves or rocks or rubber bands or something more unusual. Collecting is a great way to continue to explore similarities and differences and to sort objects into groups. Your child may decide, for example, that leaves with five points go into one box, and leaves with three points into another.

Young collectors exhibit different styles. Some collect everything; others pick and choose. "I already have an acorn with a hat on," a young specialist might remark. "Now I need one whose top has fallen off."

Some children like to sort through and group items in their collections by color, size, or texture; others turn the objects into people and things and use them to create stories.

- **Making predictions.** A major question in science is, "What will happen if . . . ?" If I mix the blue paint with the red paint? If I plant this sunflower seed? If I let go of the ball at the top of the slide? When scientists test their theories—hypotheses—they are seeing if their predictions hold up.

    Seeing what happens next does not always have to be in the form of guessing the outcome—it can also be open-ended. Sometimes you aren't at all certain *what* will happen. The important thing is to keep your eyes and your mind open. You and your child can find out together if your shadows will get longer or shorter when you walk toward the light, if the bar of soap floats or sinks, if the gelatin hardens faster in the small or large container.

- **Thinking about cause and effect.** Little children love pushing buttons and turning dials to make the radio blare, turning the lights on, and making the phone ring at Grandma's house. They are fascinated by their own effect on the objects and people around them. As a team, you can look at how one thing causes another: The wind blows the leaves; the dog knocks over his water bowl; the loud noise startles the baby; the cold in the freezer turns the water to ice.

    Noticing cause and effect can be the basis for early experimentation. If your child pours the bubble bath into the middle of the tub, nothing happens. If she dribbles it under running water, lots of bubbles form.

Experiment

Here are some activities that can constitute early science experiments:

- **Playing with pets.** Observe animal behavior and talk about it. Watching animals teaches children about basic life processes and about how animals respond to their surroundings. "Frisky always goes to sleep in the warmest corner," you might point out, or "Jaws the goldfish can tell when he's going to be fed from the tapping on his bowl."

- **Being the weatherperson.** Notice each day's weather and discuss if it's cloudy, rainy, sunny, or some combination. Look at how people dress and move in different kinds of weather. Check thermometers and barometers. Determine which way the wind is blowing by watching clouds and trees.

- **Cooking.** Working in the kitchen is one of the soundest science activities there is. What happens when foods are heated? When they are frozen? When ingredients are mixed? Children get a lot of firsthand experience with cause and effect as they boil or beat an egg or see apples turn into applesauce.

- **Becoming body conscious.** Growth charts and weight scales teach children about their favorite subject—themselves. Photo albums are another great way to trace progress. ("Was that me?")

  Young experimenters can make hand- and footprints with paint and then compare left hand to right hand or handprints to footprints.

  Noticing similarities and differences between people ("Sally has brown eyes and straight hair, Jennifer has gray eyes and curly hair") provides an opportunity to underscore how special and unique each person is.

- **Gardening.** Growing plants gives children early experiences in nurturing as well as in science. Lima beans and grapefruit seeds can be started in moist paper towels, then transferred to soil once roots start to sprout. Children can watch their plants develop and compare the amount of growth and leaf types. They can also become familiar with what plants need to thrive. Children love outdoor gardening as well, but it's important to choose seeds that yield quick results. (Try radishes or birdseed.)

Question and Explore

Young children are right in the middle of making some basic discoveries about the world: that objects fall when you drop them; that all animals need food. The best way for you to help your child learn about science is to share her enthusiasm and be available to answer questions or look for answers. Encourage her to keep her eyes and ears open, to notice and question what's happening around her, and to take an active role in exploring her environment.

How to Answer Your Child's Questions

On any day of the year, at any given moment, children the world over are asking their parents questions. Regardless of the children's backgrounds, their questions are surprisingly similar: They want to know about birth, life, and death. (Where do babies come from? If we bury a dead rabbit will it come alive again?) They wonder about adult behavior. (If it's bad to kill, why do people kill deer and other stuff? Why does Aunt Charlotte always pinch my cheek?)

They question the quirks in their language. (What's a dam? Is it like when Daddy says "Damn"?) They're curious about the unseen. (Does God eat dinner? How does Santa know where we live?) They want to know about the natural world. (Why is the sky blue? Where does rain come from?)

Most parents alternately close their ears to the umpteenth question of the day or attempt to answer each question in great detail. The philosophical stance behind each answer will be based, of course, on the parents' own belief system. What their children understand from their parents' answer will be based upon how parents respond to questions, not necessarily on how much explanation parents offer. Take, for instance, the variety of ways parents can answer one of life's easier questions: *Where does rain come from?* Each response below takes a different approach and leads each child in a different direction.

DAD: Well, Chris, the rain is from the clouds. You see, the clouds are sort of like steam when we put the kettle on. Then when it gets colder, the clouds turn to water and it rains.

CHRIS, AGE 6: But it's not cold today.

MOM: It rains because the clouds have water in them. The water that comes out is called "rain."

Angie, age 5, said nothing. A few weeks later, she and her mother were out on a cloudy day. Angie said, "Mommy, there's lots of clouds, so how come it isn't raining?"

MOM: You sound like you've been thinking about it. Why do you think it rains?

PAUL, AGE 5: I think it's to clean things off.

MOM: Rain does clean things off. Can you think of anything else it does?

DAD: What do you think, Sarah?

SARAH, AGE 4: Maybe God doesn't want me to play outside because I was bad today.

DAD: What about all the children who were good today? Do you think it's raining in their yards, too, or not?

In all of these conversations, there is one enormous plus: The parents have listened to the children's questions and treated them with respect. Children whose questions are taken seriously are likely to keep asking them. But beyond the fact that they all listened, the parents differed considerably in their approaches to the same question.

Telling the Child

Chris's father did a lot of telling. He began by trying to explain clouds in terms of something his son might know about—steam from the kettle. Though it is a good idea to use familiar experiences to help children understand natural phenomena like clouds, it probably didn't work in this instance. The connection between the steam over the kitchen stove and the solid-looking masses of clouds up in the sky is a pretty difficult one for a young child to see.

Chris's father might have first asked some questions to see if Chris had ever noticed the steam from a kettle. Instead, he went on to more elaborate explaining. When it gets colder, he pointed out, clouds turn to rain. Now Chris was really confused. (It's a warm day; it's raining a lot, and you said that cold makes rain!) The concept of relative cold is too difficult for the typical six-year-old.

It's easy to misjudge what a child can understand, particularly when you're doing all the talking. When a parent pours out an explanation without any reaction from the child, he is operating totally in the dark about what the child knows and is able to understand.

How about Angie's mother? She was also a "teller," but she did a much better job of taking into account her child's level of understanding. She did not try to explain the entire causal sequence of rain; she just told Angie its immediate source—that is, clouds. Often we assume the child's question asks for more than it does. When dealing with young children, it's good to keep your response simple and allow the child to inquire further (if she wants to) and in the direction where her interest lies.

You cannot expect a child, particularly a young child, to attain a complete understanding of a natural phenomenon, or anything else, all at once. Throughout childhood, youngsters are developing new ideas of how the world works, then discarding the ideas as they outgrow them. You are not giving the five-year-old the answer she will put on her college entrance exam—just a little information to work with as she thinks things through at her current level of reasoning.

Parents should also realize that children need time to absorb information and concepts, to make the ideas their own. When Angie's mother told her rain came from clouds, that was new information for her. From then on, when Angie saw rain, she often thought about the clouds it came from. For several weeks, that was that. Then one day she looked up at the clouds and wondered why there were clouds and no rain. At that point, Angie was ready for more, ready in a way she wouldn't have been if her mother had tried to give her the whole story at once.

The next two parents, instead of starting right in with answers, tried to find out what the children were thinking.

What Paul was asking, it turned out, was, "What is rain for? What purpose does it serve?" Because his mother asked him his ideas first, she discovered this—and, as a result, their conversation continued about the functions of rain. By referring the question back to Paul, his mother also put him in the position of having to think about his ideas and put them into words. So Paul did more active thinking than he would have had his mother given her response immediately. Once they had talked about the things Paul had noticed rain doing, his mother could then go on to give him further information about the subject.

When Sarah asked about rain, she was thinking in very personal terms. This is very common with children under six, who see the world largely in terms of themselves. An explanation of the physical causes of rain would not have been pertinent. But her father's query—"Was it raining on the children who had been good?"—was right on target. It set Sarah thinking, because it was directly relevant to what was on her mind.

Be a Good Listener

Much of the key to handling children's questions well lies simply in listening to them. But there are some specific things parents should listen for. Remember to:

- **Find out what your child is really asking.** It may not always be what you think. Let her explain what she wants to know.

- **Find out what ideas and information she already has on the subject.** To give a useful response, you need to know your child's starting point, her current "theories."

- **Keep your answers simple.** Your child needs time to take in new information and concepts. She can always ask for more when she's ready.

- **Let your child see you being curious about the world,** both through your interested responses to her questions and through hearing you wonder and inquire.

- **Develop an atmosphere in which your child feels comfortable exploring and raising questions with you.** Treat the situation as something that the two of you (or the whole family) are going to discuss, rather than as a topic on which you are going to inform your child.

Don't forget that it isn't as important for your child to understand a subject—rain or whatever—immediately as it is for her to grow up curious and reflective. Inquiring minds thrive where there is lots of dialogue and discussion and a minimum of one-sided lectures. A let's-think-about-this style of responding to children's questions is a good foundation for a lifetime of talking things over together. And the child who learns to question the world is likely to grow up with a great desire to learn throughout her life.

CHAPTER EIGHT

• • • • • •

The Arts

The Visual Arts: How Children Solve Problems Through Artwork

The artist has a problem. He is struggling to achieve a likeness of something he has never drawn before: a duck in flight. He is pleased with the head but cannot achieve an equally good rendering of the aft section. Ah, he's adding something—a cloud through which the duck is flying. His furrowed brow relaxes. Pleased with the addition, he comments, "His bottom doesn't show 'cause it's inside the clouds."

Brian, the artist, is a typical five-year-old. He has shown impressive ingenuity here, but no more so than other young children show as they confront the tough challenges of drawing. The difficulty is partly caused by the child's limited motor coordination. But the real challenge for each child is that he must invent for himself ways of showing the people, things, and events of his world on the flat page. It is not a matter of copying. It is a matter of inventing, of analyzing objects and actions into components; it is really about solving problems. And in drawing, children's problem-solving processes are visible, so we find out a great deal about how they think about and deal with the world.

Solutions like Brian's are particularly revealing. His decision to hide part of the duck in the clouds tells us a lot about what he understands. He clearly knows what is hard for him and when he is not meeting with success. Realizing he has a problem, Brian uses his knowledge of the world to bail himself out. He puts to use a number of things he knows—that clouds are in the sky, that they are soft enough to be penetrated, that an object is partially hidden from sight as it passes behind a mass like a cloud. Brian's neat solution to his problem of drawing the duck's behind is based on such past knowledge. It is a genuine act of invention that rests on the shoulders of dozens of prior inventions.

How Drawings Show Development

The circle that Brian used for the duck's head was the first enclosed form that he mastered. It evolved out of his circular scribblings and proved to be a useful tool for almost anything he drew—a flower, a car, a dog, a person. In drawing people and animals, children often begin by adding to a circle some lines for arms and legs. At first the limbs protrude directly from the head. Gradually, children add various amenities such as ears, mouths, and hair. They practice drawing people over and over, working out new solutions and refinements, using these until they are smooth and easy and then moving on.

Development never rests. No sooner does the child learn to draw a human figure to his satisfaction than he takes on new challenges, such as trying to make Mommy look different from Daddy or drawing big brother kicking a ball. In action drawings, we get a good view of children's capacity for imaginative problem-solving and the bumpy-but-persistent course of their development. Young children have great difficulty making any of the adjustments needed to depict the human figure in various positions like bending, throwing, or sitting. A number of researchers have asked children to draw a child picking up a ball on the ground. Preschool and kindergarten children in Princeton, New Jersey, tackled the problem in a variety of ways.

One popular solution was old "Gorilla Arm." The boy needs to reach all the way to the floor, so why not give him a nice long arm? Another favorite was the L-shaped limb, similar to the gorilla arm in that expediency reigns and proportion takes a beating.

Other solutions were reminiscent of Brian's cloud-shrouded duck. Sam put the boy standing on his head to pick up the ball. Liza declared, "I'm making the ball as tall as the boy." Karla put her ball on a table, bringing it to a more convenient height. And Teddy said, "My guy is catching it as it bounces up." The ingenious human mind, in a five-year-old version!

Sam, Liza, Karla, and Teddy each dealt with a difficult design problem by clever sidestepping. Their maneuvers will not satisfy them forever. They simply know what they can do at this point, and they work out their strategies accordingly. For the parent, noticing the places where a child wiggles through the cracks can be as informative as looking at any of his other achievements—and as impressive.

What Should the Parent Be Doing?

When parents become aware that drawing is far from a mindless activity, they often ask two questions: "How do I know if my child's development is up to par?" and "What should I be doing?" Though easily overemphasized, these are valid concerns, and the more intrigued parents become by their children's drawing, the more curious they are about the answers.

Some children draw better than others. Does that mean that these children are more intellectually advanced? Definitely not. Problem solving is heavily involved in children's art, but it is the problem-solving processes, not the finished products, that reflect mental growth. A great deal of thought and creativity is involved in drawing even when the results are less than imposing.

At the Educational Testing Service, the drawings of a gifted preschool class were studied. The children's comments about what they were *trying* to accomplish were often unusually reflective or original. But the gifted children's houses were as misshapen and their dogs as rough-hewn as those of their peers. Children's fine motor skills develop at different rates, and drawings themselves do not mirror intellectual development.

So the drawings are not the important thing. But is there anything parents can do to nurture the inventiveness, the persistence, or the zest with which children approach drawing? The most important thing is to stand back and enjoy. Beyond that there are a few pointers to help create a fertile atmosphere for children's drawing adventures:

Give your child a chance to tell you about his picture. Children nearly always have more in mind than they can manage to draw. Sometimes they are frustrated by the gap between what they are trying to create and what they can actually achieve. Their verbal descriptions can help close this gap.

Don't solve your child's problems for him. When your child hits a rough spot, avoid the temptation to show him or tell him how to proceed. Instead, let him know that it is his effort and thoughtfulness that matter, not the smoothness of the finished product.

Encourage playfulness and experimentation. Drawing

thrives where there is a freewheeling, playful spirit. Children pick up from you the sense that it's fun to try different approaches, to experiment, and to look for alternatives.

Make materials accessible to the child. Art materials need not be fancy, but they should be readily available to the child even when you're not.

Make only genuine and open-ended suggestions. You might say, ''We had so much fun at the zoo. Maybe you'd like to draw a picture of something about our day.'' Offer a genuine suggestion, don't give a directive. The child should feel no pressure to take up the idea if it doesn't interest him.

In such ways as these, you communicate that you value drawing and that you enjoy seeing and hearing about your child's creations. Within this atmosphere, the natural forces of development will take over. You can relax and enjoy. It is not by chance that children all over the world draw pictures—with a stick in the dirt, with a finger on the window frost. It is fun for them to see the marks they make, to be in control. It is important and exciting for them to find ways of representing the people and things they see. Be relieved that you don't have to motivate or monitor this process. It has its own momentum and its own remarkable course.

By fits and starts, the child moves forward in the absorbing task of putting things in the world on paper. As you watch and listen to this process, you'll continually find surprising nuggets. And the next time your child gives you a drawing of an eight-legged horse or a pear-shaped mommy, you can feel absolutely justified in thinking it's a marvel. There on paper you have a stop-frame glimpse of something worthy of awe—a developing human mind.

• •

Fun and Games in an Art Museum

Sharing art provides a special time together for both parent and child. Communicating about the meaning and worth of an artwork can also result in learning about and respecting another family member's views and feelings.

Because each work offers many possible meanings, attempting to understand an art object will enhance your child's creative abilities.

Enthusiasm and a sense of adventure are all you need to take your kids to a museum or an exhibit. While a knowledge of art history may be valuable to adults, a lecture-style presentation only bores youngsters.

Games aren't boring, though, and special activities designed to be used by youngsters while visiting a museum can provide an ideal way to introduce art appreciation, which includes understanding what ideas, feelings, or stories a particular piece communicates. Playing games puts the emphasis on enjoyment—where it belongs.

Remember that the ages suggested for the following games are guidelines, not absolutes. And for any visit, just choose two or three games to play.

Find That Painting
(ages 4 and up)

Upon arrival, go first to the gift shop and ask a clerk to show you which postcard reproductions represent paintings and sculptures that are currently on display. Let your child choose a few cards that appeal to him and make a game of finding those works and learning more about them.

At home, he might want to make up an album or scrapbook for collecting these inexpensive reproductions.

Who's Got the Color?
(ages 4 and up)

Before the trip, cut out four-inch squares of colors from construction paper. At the museum, give out the squares and let the children find paintings done in "their" colors.

Hidden Shapes
(ages 5 and up)

From black, gray, or white construction paper, cut out a circle, oval, square, rectangle, triangle, and half-circle. Give two or three shapes to each child and ask him or her to find similar shapes in paintings, sculptures, and other works.

With older kids, explain that artists often arrange people in groups that form trianglelike shapes. Ask your youngsters to look for the shapes that groups of people can form.

What's in a Name?
(ages 5 and up)

Choose a painting or have your child pick a favorite. Read the title and then ask, "Why do you think the artist named it that?" Suggest that your child think up a better, more descriptive, or funnier title. This works especially well with abstract works, and it will certainly encourage creativity.

Tactile Textures
(ages 6 and up)

When viewing paintings, discuss texture. Begin with, "If you could touch the painting, would it feel rough or smooth?" In realistic painting, point out how well the artist portrays things like the silky cloth of a woman's dress or the roughness of old wood.

Be sure your child looks rather than touches. Guards will speak sternly to a child if a work of art is touched. Many museums have lasers that set off a loud alarm when a person gets too close. Either experience can be upsetting to a young child.

The Story Hour
(all ages)

Realistic artists often want to communicate a story to the viewer; artists are, after all, storytellers. Children might like to consider what the artist is "saying."

After your excursion, sit down together, choose a postcard, and ask your child to make up a story about the event or place pictured. You might begin by asking, "What do you think is happening in this picture?"

Here are some additional points to consider when planning your trip:

Allow plenty of time. Your children will enjoy their visit more if it's the first stop of the day and they're fresh.

Small groups are best for viewing art. Don't take the entire neighborhood.

Try to be open-minded about unusual works of art. Lacking preconceived ideas about art, most youngsters are wonderfully receptive to experimental works. Your negative comments could limit their enjoyment.

Inquire about programs for children. Many museums have exhibits designed just for kids where they can touch works and manipulate materials.

● ●

Making Music Together

It's easy to recognize that children the world over are interested in and capable of producing visual artwork. We readily supply them with paper and crayons and encourage their efforts. When it comes to music, however, we tend to think that a certain "talent" must be there before we begin to encourage any musical exploration, or it may simply be that we'd rather see our children quietly painting than hear them practice on their drum sets. But helping children develop musical appreciation does not require that they have any particular musical talent, nor does it mean that your child needs to take lessons on a musical instrument. Appreciating music can be a pursuit you can share with your child and one that can bring a great deal of pleasure into both your lives.

Working together to make instruments is one way to bring an appreciation of sound to your children: A sealed oatmeal box with dried beans inside becomes a shaker; a coffee can is a drum and spoons are the sticks; pot lids can be very effective—and earsplitting—cymbals. With older preschoolers, you can try making a zither by stretching rubber bands across a wooden cigar box or experiment with a row of glasses filled with different levels of water, which will make different tones when tapped—gently—with a spoon.

Though it may not seem like Introduction to Music 101, sharing lullabies, chants, and songs like "This Little Piggy Went to Market," "Ride a Cock Horse to Banbury Cross," "Ring Around a Rosy," and "Pop! Goes the Weasel" helps to give children a good feeling about music. Play *your* favorite music and explain, when your child is old enough to understand, why you like it and how it makes you feel.

Discuss your children's favorites and explore their likes and dislikes.

When a birthday or special occasion rolls around, consider a simple cassette player as a present—it's much easier to manipulate than a record player, tapes are slightly less fragile than LPs, and youngsters enjoy the independence that comes from being able to play *what* they want, *when* they want to hear it.

Singing songs as a family—holiday songs, lullabies at bedtime—is another way to enjoy music, and musical games can be fun as well. Youngsters love songs with repetitive choruses and predictable patterns, so rounds are usually enthusiastically received. Try "Row, Row, Row Your Boat," "Three Blind Mice," and "Frere Jacques" for starters.

Kids also enjoy challenges, which helps account for the popularity of remembering songs like "Old McDonald" and "She'll Be Coming 'Round the Mountain." They also like movement and activity, which they get in tunes such as "This Old Man," "If You're Happy and You Know It, Clap Your Hands," "Bingo," and "Where is Thumbkin?"

Readiness

How can you tell if your child should start formal music lessons?

In very young children, indicative behavior may include gravitating toward the piano, paying particular attention when the stereo is on, or frequently singing at home. A child with natural ability will often comment on music he hears, saying, "Isn't that nice?" or "That sounds good!"

Taking Lessons

Children often start instrumental lessons with piano or violin, and the age at which they should begin is determined by several factors, the most important being the child's own interest. Pushing a child into formal instruction in music (or any other subject) before he's ready is likely to backfire. Not only can it lead to a child being turned off to music, it may also lead to his being turned off to himself, deflating his self-esteem instead of helping to build it.

Movement and Dance

Encouraging Children's Natural Rhythm

"Wow, that music really gets the kid dancing!" exclaimed Susan, eight-months pregnant. "Must be a hardcore bluegrass fan, just like Mom and Dad." It wasn't until she lovingly patted her stomach that her friends realized she was referring to a dancer who had not yet made his or her debut. Susan's comment—the idea that there is movement to music even in the womb—has turned out to be no old wives' tale. Scientists have now determined that fetuses do in fact respond to rhythmic sound. Pregnant women have known it all along: Music and movement go together from the start.

Throughout childhood, music is a potent and very physical force. A rock 'n' roll song often naturally sends babies into motion. Toddlers, though not notable for keeping time to the beat, will happily clap, rock, or sway when there is music on. As children approach age three, we begin to see something that looks more like dancing. Now they move roughly in time with the music. Preschool children make up little dances, sometimes dramatizing songs or events, sometimes expressing emotions or moods.

Developing Your Child's Enjoyment of Rhythm

This spontaneous and seemingly inherent desire to dance is easily encouraged. Parents can play an important role in their child's enjoyment and exploration of moving to music. Here are some of the ways you can do this:

Let the music move you—and take the child along. If you've always danced to the stereo, especially when no one was around; don't stop now. When your child is an infant, hold him in your arms as you dance—the perfect partner, he'll never step on your toes. Feeling the changes in the rhythm and tempo of your movement as the music changes, your baby will get a direct introduction to the pleasures of moving to music. And when your child is on his own two feet, keep on moving to the music, dancing separately or holding hands.

Don't feel that all the music you share with your child has to be "children's music." Play what you like, whether it's rock, disco, reggae, country, or classical. The more you are immersed in the music, the better. Watching adults dance and enjoy music is the best initiation children can have. Growing up in such an environment, as all children do in less urbanized societies, youngsters come naturally to appreciate the music and dance of their parents.

Encourage children to explore what they can do with their bodies and the different ways they can move in space. Our bodies can move in many different ways: stepping, sliding, skipping, bouncing; forward, backward, sideways, up, down; slowly, rapidly, smoothly, jerkily; limbs curling, stretching, twisting. Though children can discover much about movement on their own, parents can invite them to a fuller exploration of its possibilities and variations.

Even before you can communicate with your child verbally, you can give him new ideas for movement and spark his inclination to try out variations. Suppose the child is listening to a lively song, bouncing and clapping his hands. Dance along with him for awhile, doing what he does—he'll love that—and then introduce a change. For instance, you might start moving your head from side to side along with the beat. When you throw in new possibilities, you're bringing a playful mood to the dancing, a what-else-can-we-do-with-our-bodies spirit of exploration.

Help your children identify some of the things they do naturally. Kids are responsive to mood, rhythm, tempo, volume, and other elements of music, but they are mostly unaware of what is making them react. By pointing these things out to your children, you can increase their awareness and enjoyment. For example: Marie saw her daughter respond to tempo changes in a marching song by slowing or speeding her pace. She said, "Aimee, I see you going slow, fast, then slow again. How come?" Aimee had been changing speed without noticing why. Hearing her mother's question, she reflected, "When the music goes fast, my feet go fast." When the record ended, Marie suggested, "Let's try another record and see how it makes us feel like moving." She chose a record with dramatic changes in tempo, helping Aimee notice what was happening in the music.

Provide the child with props, including "musical instruments," for enhancing the moving-to-music experience. Try blocks of wood or sticks to tap together, bells, tambourines, drums, etc. Whether bought or improvised from household objects, these instruments add an extra element to children's pleasure in rhythmic movement.

Various nonmusical items can also enhance the experience of moving to music: a mirror; articles of clothing like capes that swirl as the child moves; perhaps a chiffon scarf to add to the drama of flowing movement. The child will be fascinated too by moving and dancing when he can see his shadow—which you can arrange by placing a strong light source (such as a bright lamp or a movie or slide projector) in a dim room.

Recognize that giving your child formal lessons at a very early age is not necessarily the best way to encourage an interest in movement and dance. Gina's parents want to give her a chance to develop her apparent affinity for dancing. Her father says, ''Since she was a year old, Gina has been dancing whenever music comes on. Now that she's older, I think it's time for her to have dance lessons.''

Are dance classes for young children a good idea? It depends on the nature of the class. You can judge by observing the teacher in action. Is the tone of the class light and fun? Are most of the children enjoying themselves, or are there just a few who seem to be able to do what the teacher wants? Is the emphasis on responding to the music and exploring what the body can do, or on learning routines and being in step? Is there a great deal of concern about preparing for a performance?

The answers to these questions are particularly important in preschool and the early grades. At this age, most children have to work hard to learn steps and sequences of steps, and they differ widely in their ability to do so. Even when they succeed, it may be at the expense of their natural grace.

If the classes focus mainly on remembering and performing steps in synchrony with peers, performing for an audience, and regular critiques by the teacher, they may end up making the child self-conscious about dance and movement. That's just the opposite of what parents want their children to gain from an early dance experience. Even when the child goes on to dance "seriously," more benefit is derived from early experiences that emphasize exploring and taking pleasure in movement, rather than the memorizing of dance routines. As the child gets older, parents may be guided in their decisions about formal instruction by the intensity of the child's interest in dancing and by evidence of some ability.

Define What You Want for Your Child

In deciding about your child's need for formal instruction, and in sharing moving-to-music experiences with your children, begin by asking yourself what you are hoping for. The child being at ease with his body? His pleasure in moving well? The development of an aesthetic appreciation of music and dance? These are all things the child first gains from the people around him. Parents, by showing their own natural enjoyment of music and dance, can give their children a gift of appreciation and encouragement that will last a lifetime. Few things, after all, are more infectious—to parent, child, anyone—than the joy of moving to music.

PART III

······

Learning and Culture

Introduction to Part III

• • • • • •

When social scientists refer to *culture*, they have a big picture in mind. They're considering all the aspects of life that people in a community share and that people themselves have created. Culture includes the relationships between children, parents, and other caretakers; the structures of authority; the kinds of work people do; their language; their religion; the tools and gadgets at their disposal; their artistic forms; the design of their buildings; and the layout of their community. The culture in which a child grows up also determines what she needs to learn to be a productive member of her particular society.

In Western culture, academic learning is a key element of success; children are judged on their ability to acquire language and mathematical skills. Thus, the inability to perform certain academic tasks can create hardships for children. By taking culture into account, however, we can see that a condition such as *dyslexia*—the scrambled perception of letters and numbers that makes it hard for some people to read, spell, and write—is actually a social problem.

In another society, dyslexia might be no problem at all, and children who had this difficulty would not be labeled "learning disabled." In a culture without the kind of written language we have, dyslexia might never even be noticed. On the other hand, most children do perfectly well in our culture without the ability to "read" the sun and

119

stars. They might be in trouble in a society where navigating the open seas was a crucial task. In the following chapters, we'll look at the social institutions involved in early learning and offer suggestions on ways to help your child reach her potential within—and sometime in spite of—these systems.

CHAPTER NINE

• • • • • •

Early Childhood Education: What Can It Provide?

Formal early education programs are proliferating, and children are attending preschool in record numbers and at increasingly younger ages. Consider these figures:

- In 1986, 38.9 percent of three- and four-year-olds were enrolled in preschool programs, according to the U.S. Census. That represents an almost sevenfold increase from 1968, when the figure was only 5.7 percent.

- During roughly the same time period, the number of nursery schools increased one thousandfold.

- Every state in the union now provides some form of public support for kindergarten. In 1965 only twenty-five states did so.

What's behind these trends? One explanation, of course, is that the necessity of a second income, the rising number of single-parent families, and expanding job opportunities for women have propelled more and more mothers into the job market. Someone must mind the children, and parents are understandably concerned that time with a caretaker be wisely spent. Appropriate preschool programs have proven to be an important way to meet the very real needs of growing numbers of families.

The Head Start programs of the early 1960s, which offered a bootstrap to children born into poverty, also left their mark by popularizing the idea that preschool can open new avenues of opportunity to all children. And it has been argued that in our highly technological society, children are sophisticated enough to benefit from training at an earlier age than in generations past. These ideas have given rise to the notion that enrolling a child in preschool will provide him with an important edge in this era of heightened competition.

But just how significant really is preschool to a child's development? Curiously, there is no firm evidence to suggest that it makes a decisive difference to most middle-class children. It is safe to conclude that whether or not a child enters a formal preschool program matters less than how appropriate his earliest learning opportunities are. The best education—whether acquired at home or in school—takes place in a supportive, loving environment and introduces a child to a range of exciting new experiences. Education that focuses primarily on academic achievements, by contrast, can unnecessarily dampen a child's natural enthusiasm for learning.

Preschool programs can provide very genuine benefits to parents. By giving them a welcome respite from the demands of child care or relieving them from concern as they head off to work, appropriate preschool programs can improve the quality of a parent's life—and that, in turn, can enhance the relationship between parent and child.

At its best, a formal preschool program contributes to a child's success in school—and later in life—by improving his concentration, acclimating him to working in a group, and training him to listen. As children learn to interact with new adults, play with toys that are different from those available at home, and relate to many children at once, they build a strong foundation of confidence and imagination.

Children who have attended preschool often find the transition to kindergarten and elementary school easier. Early education can be of particular benefit when it focuses on:

Cooperation. By playing with others a child learns the all-important skills of sharing and negotiating. By discovering that others share his fears and pleasures, a child understands that his feelings are not unique, an important step toward developing a sense of common humanity.

Independence. Because he must share his teacher's attention with many other children, a child grows more self-reliant.

Trust. When a child discovers that other adults besides his parents will care for him, he learns to feel safer in the world beyond his own home.

Communication. Interacting with other children helps a child realize he must use language to be understood.

A sense of belonging. The predictable routines and responsibilities that come with being a member of a group instill loyalty and security in a child.

Selecting a Preschool Program for Your Child

Traditionally, nursery schools have run half-day sessions and have been viewed as tools to socialize children in the year or two before they enter kindergarten or first grade.

Day-care centers, by contrast, were developed primarily to provide all-day custodial care to preschoolers of any age.

Today, however, the distinction between the role of nursery schools and day-care centers has become somewhat blurred. Nursery schools are expanding their hours and accepting children of many ages, while the best day-care centers now provide a mixture of social, artistic, and physical activities that rival many nursery-school programs. Both nursery schools and day-care centers can operate in a private home, a storefront, a church basement, a local "Y," or a community center. Although some day-care centers provide little more than group baby-sitting services, the term *preschool* is increasingly being used in a generic sense to mean any program for children not yet ready for kindergarten. On the other hand, some preschools adhere to a particular philosophy about early-childhood education.

In Search of an Appropriate Curriculum

Many experts agree that the key to the effectiveness of an early-childhood program is that it be *developmentally appropriate*. According to the National Association for the Education of Young Children (NAEYC), "Knowledge of typical development of children within the age span served by the program provides a framework from which teachers prepare the learning environment and plan appropriate experiences . . . This knowledge is used in conjunction with understanding about individual children's growth patterns, strengths, interests, and experiences to design the most appropriate learning environment."

Programs for infants and toddlers should therefore enable them to experience the environment through their senses, to move around freely, and to interact with both adults and other children. *Developmentally Appropriate Practice*, an NAEYC report, explains: "The most appropriate teaching technique for this age group is to give ample opportunities for the children to use self-initiated repetition to practice newly acquired skills and to experience feelings of autonomy and success. Infants will bat at, grasp, bang or drop their toys . . . Imitation, hiding and naming games are also important for learning at this age. Realistic toys will enable children to engage in increasingly complex types of play."

An appropriate program for three-year-olds, according to the NAEYC report, emphasizes language, activity, and movement, with major emphasis on large-muscle activity. Dramatic play, wheel toys and climbers, puzzles and blocks, and opportunities to talk and listen to simple stories are all important sources of stimulation for this age group.

Ready for an even greater variety of experiences, four-year-olds benefit from activities that help develop their small-motor skills, such as using scissors, creating artwork, and cooking. As they develop a grasp of basic math concepts and problem-solving skills, children are more able to concentrate and remember as well as to recognize objects by shape, color, or size. Some four-year-olds and most five-year-olds are also displaying a growing interest in the written language.

Above all, notes NAEYC, the developmental appropriateness of an early childhood program can be measured by the interactions between adults and children. In a preschool that is tailored to meet the needs of its children, the care-taking adults:

- Respond quickly and directly to children's needs and appreciate their differing styles and abilities.

- Provide many varied opportunities for children to communicate.

- Help children complete tasks successfully by providing support, focused attention, physical proximity, and verbal encouragement. Teachers in appropriate programs recognize that children learn from trial and error and that children's misconceptions reflect their developing thoughts.

- Are alert to signs of undue stress in children's behavior and are aware of appropriate stress-reducing activities and techniques.

- Help children develop self-esteem by demonstrating respect and acceptance at all times.

- Are responsible for all children under their supervision and plan for increasing independence as children acquire skills.

The concept of developmental appropriateness should guide parents in selecting any preschool. Whether it bears the imprint of a particular educational innovator, as do several described below, or whether it blends the best ideas from a number of theories, a good preschool is one that truly respects the ways in which children learn.

Types of Preschools

The Montessori Program

In the early 1900s, Maria Montessori, the first woman in Italy to receive a medical degree, developed an educational model based on the principle that preschool children are eager to learn and benefit most from a program that strives to develop independence and autonomy. Working first with intellectually handicapped children and later with children from the slums of Rome, Dr. Montessori pioneered the use of child-size furniture and developed a set of "auto-didactic (self-teaching) materials" to enhance a child's coordination, educate his senses, advance his use of language, and refine his understanding of the physical world. Once a child reached the age of four, he was usually introduced to preliminary reading, writing, and arithmetic skills.

Today, the Montessori label is used by thousands of schools, although its basic tenets have been interpreted in many different ways. In most Montessori programs, a child progresses at his own pace in an environment that has been equipped with an orderly and easily accessible array of special objects. To enhance physical coordination, for example, a child is given different frames that hold a piece of cloth, which can be buttoned, hooked, snapped, or tied together. To assist in reading and writing readiness, children pronounce letters of the alphabet while tracing those letters on raised sandpaper. The teacher's role is limited to that of an observer and resource person, someone who demonstrates the proper use of materials and helps a child use them in progressively more complex tasks.

An emphasis on individuality and the principle that children should be permitted to move about freely underlie the Montessori program. In *The Discovery of the Child*, Maria Montessori explains that a child should be prevented "from doing anything which may offend or hurt others or which is impolite or unbecoming. But everything else, every act that can be useful in any way whatever may be expressed. . . . It is essential that a child's spontaneous movements should not be checked or that he be compelled to act according to the will of another."

Open Classroom

The concept of the open classroom is modeled on a revolution that took place in British elementary schools after World War II. In *The Open Classroom Reader,* a compendium of writings about unconventionally structured classrooms, editor Charles Silberman emphasized that the term *open classroom—informal* or *open education* are also used—is not precisely defined but represents instead a set of convictions about the nature of teaching and learning. According to Sir Alec Clegg, a leading educational innovator and author of *Revolution in the British Primary Schools,* the objective of the open classroom ". . . is not so much to convey knowledge as it is to excite a determination in the child to acquire it for himself and to teach him how to go about acquiring it."

An open classroom is usually arranged to allow children to work in groups or alone, rather than sitting in rows of desks. The teacher is essentially a facilitator who encourages children to seek out knowledge, not an all-knowing authority figure who simply hands it to them. Rigid schedules and the use of worksheets are minimized, and the structure of the day is as fluid as possible. The basis of learning depends less on drills and more on active experience.

While these represent momentous changes at the elementary level, they do not significantly differ from the pattern of activity in most nursery-school programs. Given the trend toward increasingly structured education at ever earlier ages, however, it is well worth understanding the concept of the open classroom and the respect it has been accorded. Open-classroom enthusiasts are telling us that elementary schools should be more like nursery schools—and not the other way around!

Cooperative Preschools

In a cooperative preschool, a group of parents determine the structure of a program, usually through a representative board, establish a fee structure, hire a qualified teacher, and ordinarily serve as her assistants. Parents who cannot or choose not to donate their time to the cooperative are often permitted to make additional financial contributions instead. The daily activities of a cooperative preschool are much like those of any other nursery program.

Play Groups

Despite all our talk of formal early education, the fact is that the majority of young children are still cared for in their homes by parents, another relative, or an informal network of friends until they reach kindergarten age. One informal way that parents extend the learning opportunities available to them is through play groups, which usually meet in the homes of the participants. Like cooperative preschools, they provide a varied play experience for children and afford parents a chance to spend time together.

Choosing a Preschool

Choosing a preschool can be a confusing venture. Faced with a variety of programs and philosophies, parents may feel intimidated: Who am I, with no training in early-childhood education, to presume to judge this school? Although this feeling may be natural, it underestimates your role. As a parent, you know more about how your child reacts to people and situations than any professional does.

If you visit several schools, you will be able to develop a keen sense of what will be good for your child.

The state licensing agency or a local child-care resource and referral service may be able to give you a list of schools in your area and basic information—ages of children enrolled, hours, and fees. You may also want to contact the National Association for the Education of Young Children, in Washington, D. C., to find out if there are any *accredited* child-care programs in your area. The NAEYC sponsors a nationwide accreditation program in which early childhood specialists assess child care sites on the basis of 150 criteria.

Pick some of the programs you've learned about, then phone and ask to visit. Good programs will welcome a parent's visit both before and after a child is enrolled. On your first visit, it's better not to take your child, unless it's requested. After you have narrowed down your choices, you and your child can visit the places you like.

Watch for Key Episodes

On your visit, make sure you see a child-filled classroom. As you sit hunched on a little chair, trying to be as inconspicuous as possible, can you really observe anything significant? Absolutely! Researchers for the Boston Children's Hospital Child Development Unit found that a judgment made after a two- or three-hour visit would be the same as one formed after an in-depth study made over two or three days—if *key episodes* were carefully observed. These key episodes are:

Arrival/departure. How do children feel about coming or leaving? How do parents and staff relate? Does the staff treat parents as partners? At the best programs, transitional times are happy times.

Snack or lunch. Can the children choose where to sit? Do they help serve and clean up? Do teachers sit with children? Eating is a social experience and should be a time of interaction.

Indoor activities. This is an opportunity to note how the teachers manage their classroom and how the staff work together. Are children forced to participate in activities? What happens when a child loses interest? Do teachers take time with children on a one-to-one basis? No child should be allowed to feel stressed or alone.

Outdoor activities. Are running, jumping, and letting off steam allowed? Are girls as well as boys encouraged to be active? Is there space indoors for rainy-day active play? Steer clear of programs that ignore a child's need for physical play.

Transition from one activity to another. Are children allowed to finish what they are doing before they are expected to go on to something else? Are children restless or bored between activities?

Discipline. What kinds of behavior are seen as problems? What does the staff do about a lonely or crying child, a fighting child, or a toilet accident? Spanking or hitting children is *not* good discipline.

Consoling/comforting. After a clash, are both the wrongdoer and the "victim" handled satisfactorily? Both should emerge with their self-esteem enhanced, not diminished.

Other Important Factors

Some other things you might look for are:

Number of children and adults. The National Day Care Study found that a maximum of about eighteen preschool children per head teacher and assistant is important for quality. There should be a head teacher and an assistant with each age group.

Physical space. The space should be roomy. Is it divided into different activity areas? You should see space and materials for play with blocks, for looking at books, and for doing artwork. There should also be special places for small table games and housekeeping. Are play materials readily available to children, and are they stored at child level?

Questions for the director. Ask to see the license or the NAEYC accreditation. These indicate that the program has passed inspections for safe premises and that it has enough trained staff. If the school is not licensed or accredited, ask if it is in the process of meeting standards. Ask about the educational philosophy. Ask the director about other things that may matter to you, such as holiday observances, nonsexist curriculum, bilingual programs, mainstreaming of handicapped children, or a policy of nondiscrimination.

The center's approach should all add up to happy, active, and involved children. As you reflect on your observations, ask yourself if you enjoyed the program and if you think your child would enjoy it day-in and day-out. The most important thing you want from a preschool is a gut feeling that it is a good place for your child.

What Do the Best Kindergarten Programs Offer?

Unlike preschool programs, which are generally independent of the local school system, kindergarten is usually an integral part, the first formal step, in a child's academic career. While the curriculum can vary greatly from school district to school district, from school to school, and even within a school, there are certain approaches that the best programs have in common:

They provide for hands-on learning. Since young children learn most easily through their own activity, the best kindergarten programs provide the chance for children to build with blocks, to paint, and to work with clay as well as to be given a chance to use structured materials, such as puzzles, and unstructured materials, such as water and sand. Many classrooms are set up with activity areas so children can work individually or in groups, finding out for themselves about the qualities of modeling clay or about what happens when you mix blue and yellow paints.

Children who are given these chances to experiment learn more about the world than they would from any formal science lesson.

They encourage interaction. The hands-on learning kindergarteners engage in requires a lot of interplay among children. Standing at the threshold of formal school, kindergarten children need to learn cooperation, turn-taking, and a number of other social skills. Under the guidance of a skilled teacher, five-year-olds can learn to follow directions, express their own needs, and respect the rights of others in a very natural and even playful way.

They respect the child's need to play. Play is often referred to as "children's work." Kindergarten programs that understand the developmental needs of five-year-olds make certain that play is an integral part of learning. While some adults may dismiss play as a frivolous waste of time for a five-year-old who has finally entered "real school," many thoughtful psychologists and educators warn that pushing a child into academics at this age is highly counterproductive. Play, on the other hand, gives children a chance to try out options, to make meaningful choices, and to practice new skills without getting bored. Play puts learning in a context and gives learning a purpose.

Children acquire many skills in kindergarten as part of their play. The letters of the alphabet, for instance, are learned as children make birthday cards for a classmate. Children may learn about numbers as they count the number of people who are in class that day or measure how much flour to use in making bread. But the emphasis should be on the playing, not on the acquisition of academic skills.

They teach a sense of community. Most kindergarten programs are set up to give children a sense of their responsibility to the community of the classroom. Children rotate such jobs as watering the plants, feeding the gerbil, and sponging the table after snacktime. Their contributions give them pride in their classroom and insight into how the group functions. Each child also takes on certain individual responsibilities—for hanging his jacket in the cubby and for putting away the crayons after using them, for example.

Kindergarten is also a time to explore the community beyond the classroom. Programs that make field trips an important part of the curriculum will, quite naturally, broaden a child's perspective. Children visit such places as the fire station, the post office, and the local pet store to learn more about the larger world. When children get back to the classroom, they can discuss the trip and re-create the place visited with building blocks or with drawings to bring home. They may even make their own wall poster or book describing the trip or learn to write a thank-you letter to the local fire captain.

They introduce the joy of literature. In well-designed kindergarten programs, books are introduced to children not as texts to be deciphered but as windows to the world. As children make their own books, using drawings, words, or other symbols, they learn the art of communicating their ideas. Most kindergartens have book corners that also encourage children to look at books on their own. And as kindergarten teachers read books aloud to their classes, they help children develop an appreciation for literature.

A lot of learning goes on in kindergarten. But most early-childhood educators would agree that what's most important is not *what* is learned but *how* it is learned. A kindergarten curriculum that sets the stage for positive attitudes about school and learning is likely to produce children who know that learning is fun, meaningful, and rewarding. These children are off to a great start.

CHAPTER TEN

• • • • • •

Getting Ready
for Grade School

Eventually, the time does come when it is appropriate for a child to enter the academic environment of elementary school. When the classroom doors open on that momentous occasion, a world of new challenges and new opportunities will lie before her. Most likely, the day's activities will be more tightly structured than in the past—although a good elementary-school program still allows plenty of time for spontaneous activities: play, arts and crafts, and show 'n' tell. The teacher-pupil ratio is likely to be higher than it was in nursery school or kindergarten, and the hours spent away from home will probably be longer. In addition, the child's school environment may be more competitive than in the past and, for the first time, she may be graded on her work.

This chapter looks at the "school readiness" skills that enable a child to thrive in that changed environment. School readiness simply refers to the set of skills and level of maturity that a child is generally expected to have before beginning elementary school.

What Do Primary-School Teachers Expect?

A healthy respect for individual learning styles and pacing is as important in elementary school—and indeed throughout a child's academic career—as it is in preschool. Realistically,

137

though, larger class sizes make it more difficult to custom-tailor education to each student's needs. That's why it is convenient and useful for students beginning first grade to have at least a baseline of skills in common.

Some of these skills are practical necessities—teachers can't accompany every child to the bathroom each time it is necessary, so everyone should know how to use the toilet and how to wash up without help. Basic social skills are also important, and a first-grader should be able to articulate her needs and relate to other children.

Here are some of the other practical skills that will help your child thrive in her earliest years of formal schooling:

- For her safety and your own peace of mind, a child should have her first and last name, address, and telephone number memorized.

- A child should be able to get dressed and undressed without assistance so that she can put on her jacket or sweater to play outside and take her shoes on and off when necessary. That means knowing how to use buttons, snaps, and zippers and how to tie—or velcro—her own shoes.

- Your child should be able to meet the rules of neatness that each teacher establishes in her classroom. She should know how to clean up a mess and put away her toys or books after use.

- A degree of emotional maturity and a number of successful experiences away from home—and in the company of other children—are important to school adjustment. Although concepts such as sharing and taking turns are emphasized in the first years of elementary school, it helps if she has already been introduced to them.

- Your child should be able to be comfortable with other adults—friends, neighbors, or the parents of playmates—

and relatively relaxed in the presence of people who are new to her. She should also recognize and respect figures of authority.

Other Components of School Readiness

A child should *not* be readied for school through drills, rote exercises, or memorization. Rather, she needs to be raised in a stimulating environment, given age-appropriate toys to play with, and the freedom to experiment. With the help of her parents, such a child will internalize many—if not most—of the skills that serve as a foundation for academics, such as:

Sizes, shapes, and numerical relationships. Familiarity with words such as *small, large, long,* and *short* and the ability to make size comparisons—for example, "his house is *bigger* than mine"—prepare a child to identify similarities and differences between objects. A child who can also distinguish common shapes, such as squares, circles, and triangles, and can draw or trace those shapes, will find it easier to begin copying letters and words than the child who does not have this background.

When she enters school, a child can probably match objects on a one-to-one basis, knowing for example that at dinner time, Mommy, Daddy, and brother need one plate, one napkin, and one fork apiece. She is also likely to be able to distinguish between *empty* and *full* and *more* or *less*. These abilities will be helpful when the time comes to learn addition and subtraction.

Colors. Identifying the three primary colors—red, blue, and yellow—is important, and many children can also identify other simple colors. By the time they enter school, most children will also be comfortable using crayons and chalk, both valuable tools of creative expression.

Position and direction. Locating objects in relation to one another—*above, below, next to, in front of*—and pinpointing directions—such as *up, down,* and *straight ahead*—contribute to a child's capacity to follow instructions, participate in group activities, and complete workbook exercises. Later, a conceptual grasp of position and direction also enables a child to think abstractly and visualize a three-dimensional world.

Time. A basic grasp of time—the fact that it passes, how different things fill shorter or longer periods, and how routine activities are structured into segments of time—helps a child understand the nature of change and repetition. Learning to wait is an important social skill that becomes easier once a child understands that her turn comes after a certain period of time passes.

Most teachers also assume that elementary-school children recognize the daylight-nighttime pattern and know their own age and date of birth.

Listening. Children learn best when they begin school with some ability to sit still and listen. Beginning first-graders should be able to concentrate long enough to understand a short story that is read aloud and should then be able to retell it in proper sequence. They also should be able to name common sounds, such as a dog barking or a fire-engine siren, and repeat phrases or lists of numbers that they hear.

Motor skills. Coordination and balance are part of a non-disabled child's normal development, and both gross and fine motor skills are critical. By the time she enters school, a child should be able to run, skip, hop, balance on one leg, descend a set of stairs by alternating one foot at a time, walk backwards, throw a ball—and still have energy left to burn on the playground. She should also have sufficient control over her smaller muscles so that she can color, cut with scissors, trace shapes, build with blocks, and touch one finger to the other.

Prereading and prewriting skills. Learning to read and write, like learning to listen and speak, are a natural part of language development. In a stimulating home environment, a child is surrounded by language—in the form of the written and spoken word—and gradually becomes aware of its importance long before she enters school.

Despite the rush-to-read trend that has penetrated some preschools, research suggests there are no long-term advantages to teaching reading to a child prior to elementary school. A more important role for parents is to generate a curiosity about words and language that will prepare children for formal lessons. By talking regularly to their infants and small children, parents can help them recognize that things have names and people communicate with sounds that have meaning. Playing word games, singing songs, asking questions, and listening carefully to the answers are all part of that recognition process.

Reading regularly to children and giving them picture books of their own stimulate their imaginations and help them view reading as relaxing and fun. Before a child enters school, she should be comfortable with books and have a small library of her own. Parents can cultivate the visual skills appropriate for reading by giving children illustrated books to thumb through and encouraging them to make up stories that match a picture they are shown.

By the time a child is actually ready to read and write she will have developed a number of fairly sophisticated auditory, visual, and motor skills. The capacity to recognize common sounds and to distinguish among consonants such as "t" and "d", the ability to distinguish left from right and to identify shapes, the dexterity required to hold a pen or pencil, and the eye-hand coordination needed to copy or trace letters are all basic prereading and prewriting skills. Generally, a child who is ready to read and write will be able to grasp the main idea of a story that is read aloud and paraphrase its main events. She will also be familiar with the appearance of the alphabet and know that words are composed of letters.

By mastering at least some of the skills of school readiness, then, your child is likely to be independent enough, and emotionally and intellectually mature enough, to adapt to and thrive in the grade-school environment. One caution for parents, though: While it is important to understand the concept of school readiness, the skills described are intended as guidelines, not as a checklist. If your child knows about colors, shapes, and position but hasn't mastered the concept of time, don't worry that she'll lag behind the others. If she's got her sense of time down but just won't sit still, again, don't be overly concerned. School, after all, has traditionally been our society's greatest institution for socialization. Your support and encouragement, combined with the care a good teacher provides, will enable your child to meet the challenges of her new academic career.

Next, we'll take a look at handling the practical and emotional aspects of the first day of school.

The First Goodbye: Easing Your Child's Starting-School Jitters

Charles is clinging to his father's leg like a drowning man grasping a lifeline. Sarah begins to wail every time her mother starts to leave. On the other side of the room, Lisa is holding a book with one hand and clutching her well-worn teddy bear with the other. Russell can be seen dogging the teacher's steps, taking her hand whenever he can. And Tony is in the block corner, hitting anyone who comes near his building.

Yesterday, these were happy, well-behaved children. What's different today?

It's the first day of school.

Not every child is going to react with fear or misbehavior when school begins. In fact, for many kids the transition from day care or home or kindergarten to first grade is fairly uneventful. But every child *will* feel a combination of emotions when school starts. She is leaving the safety and familiarity of a situation focused primarily on her emotional needs and is stepping into a world that is new and far more structured. This can be frightening, even overwhelming.

At home, children had a flexible routine: They were fed when hungry, they rested when tired. They had their own toys around them and the lion's share of adults' attention. But on the first day of school, this secure environment is left behind.

To the adult, the classroom looks enticing and inviting (toys! kids! pads! crayons!). But to the child, it presents a whole new set of rules and conventions to learn. And what's more, her mother proposes to leave her there! How does she know she's coming back? Why is she doing this to her?

Anger, fear, and uncertainty are all normal reactions to separation from familiar people, places, and routines. This entry into a new world is a big transition for a child.

Children who have attended day care may be more familiar with school conventions, but they, too, have to make adjustments when school starts. Moving from day care to school means dealing with a new teacher, new kids, and a host of new experiences.

Parents *can* make this transition smoother. Here are a number of tried-and-true tips that should help ease the initial days for your first-time-in-school child.

Before School Starts

Here are some things you can plan on doing in the weeks prior to the beginning of classes:

- **Visit the school.** One way to overcome your child's fear of the unknown is to make it known. The easiest way to do this is to schedule a trip to your child's new school *before* classes begin.

  Some schools offer planned orientation sessions. If your child's school does, take advantage of it. If no formal orientation is offered, try to arrange a meeting for you and your child with the teacher.

  You might think it wiser to visit during a regular class session. But under those circumstances, your child would have less time to explore and get to know the teacher. Besides, the sight of twenty children playing full tilt may be intimidating. Seeing the empty classroom and an unhurried teacher is a more relaxed introduction to the setting.

  Spend a little time looking around and talking with your son or daughter about what goes on in various parts of the room and school. One mother brought a camera and took photographs of each area of the school classroom and playground. Then she helped her daughter, Amy, make a "scrapbook" of her new school. With the photographs and a schedule supplied by the teacher, Amy and her mother "walked through" a sample day and talked about what Amy would be doing at school.

- **Read books about school with your child.** Reading books on starting school is excellent not only for giving your child some ideas of what to expect but also for helping her express some of her own fears and uncertainties.

- **If possible, arrange for your child to meet children who will be in her class.** Ask beforehand who will be in your child's class (or your carpool) and invite one or two of them to play at your house before the first day of school.

- **Find out in advance how the teacher handles the first weeks of school.** Does the teacher have a phase-in schedule for your child? Are mothers and fathers welcome to stay the first day or days? Some schools want the parents more or less to drop the child at the classroom door. There are, however, many starting-school programs that believe in the child making a gradual adjustment to the classroom. Often, these programs welcome having parents around—unobtrusively, of course—for a day or two.

  Working parents should plan to take leave-time during the child's first week at school so they can spend some time in the class and be able to leave when their child is ready, not because they have to get to work.

- **Make plans the night before.** For example, lay out your child's clothing with her. It might be nice to plan for your child to wear something special, or particularly comfortable, for the first day.

On the First Day

When the day arrives, there are a number of things you can do to help it go as smoothly as possible.

- **Let your child take a favorite toy to school if she wants to.** A child's separation pangs may be eased by the presence of a favorite toy. Just having a familiar "friend" along gives the child a feeling of safety and continuity. A prized possession can also be a catalyst for conversation when the child shows it to peers. (One warning, however: Not all teachers will approve of this, so be sure to ask beforehand.)

- **Be prompt.** Arriving in good time may take special effort and planning, especially on those hurried first days of school. But when a child arrives, coattails flying and tense from being rushed, and finds a whole roomful of children in the midst of play or a group activity, she is likely to be more anxious and intimidated than necessary.

  Being prompt is important at the day's end, too. As soon as mothers and fathers begin arriving to pick up their children, the child wonders where *her* mom or dad is. If you're the last parent to arrive, your child may feel abandoned and may not want to repeat the experience tomorrow.

In the Classroom

In the classroom, parents should be casual. Teachers often invite parents to participate in the activities of the class. If this is not the case in the classroom you're in, it might be helpful to take a book or magazine with you. You will *want* to watch your child's every move, but she will know if you do. If you're involved in your own reading, the child can reassure herself that you're there—without feeling anxiety focused on her.

What about a child that clings and will not leave your side? Parents sometimes feel they should firmly rebuff such clinging: ''Be a big boy now. Go play with the other children.'' Other parents, having their own difficulty with the separation, reinforce their children's clinging. The most effective approach is to provide reassurance but also convey a matter-of-fact assumption that the child will soon join the rest of the class: ''OK, Timmy, let's have a hug. Now why don't you choose one book for us to read? Then I'm going to read my magazine while you play.''

- **When you leave the classroom, let your child know.** Whether it is the first day of school or the fifth, the time will come when you need to leave. Your child may not have given you a glance for an hour, but the actual departure is another matter. Parents sometimes think they should leave unobserved. But ''slipping out'' creates more problems than it solves. When your child realizes you are gone, she will feel abandoned. And since you left when she wasn't looking, she may become afraid to let you out of her sight. It is important to tell your child that you are leaving.

- **Be very specific about where you will be and when you will be coming back.** A statement such as this is helpful: ''I'm going to the store to buy a few things for our supper. I'll be back in an hour. Miss Lacey says you'll be playing outside then, so I'll come to the playground to pick you up.'' By giving the child a mental image of what you will be doing and of your return, you give her something concrete to hold on to. Your coming back has reality, and she knows when to expect you.

What About Your Other Children?

Parents should recognize that when one child in a family starts school, all the children in the family are affected. An older sibling may resent all the attention the "novice" is getting or the fact that she herself is no longer the only "big kid" in the family. She may express this resentment by making fun of the younger child ("You're only in first grade—that's baby school!") or trying to frighten her sibling ("If you do anything wrong, you'll get sent to the principal's office.").

Try to head off galloping resentment by asking the older child to help you: "Your brother hasn't been to school yet. Why don't you tell him some of the things you like doing in school?"

Younger siblings left behind at home will need special attention during this time. Suddenly they've lost a playmate; they have a separation to deal with, too. Try to make some extra time to spend with the left-behind child.

Whatever you do, be ready to share the child's excitement, along with the uncertainties and adjustments. For parents, watching a child move beyond the threshold of the home is bound to bring some fears as well as a sense of loss. But there is also pride, shared excitement, and joy in the child's growth.

This won't be the last time you watch your child go on to wider horizons. Nor will it be the last time you remind yourself that as parents we do what we can . . . and then we let go.

Standardized Testing

No adult who has ever passed through the American school system is likely to forget the spate of standardized tests to which she was subjected. Remember the countless open circles that filled our answer sheets and the selection of freshly sharpened No. 2 pencils that we carried with us to the silent testing room? Decades later, most of us are also likely to recall, perhaps with grim amusement, how the clock ticked away until the teacher called out sharply, "Stop. Put your pencils down. Do not begin the next section until you are told to do so."

Much has changed since then, but it is still customary for students to take a battery of I.Q. and other standardized tests in the years between school enrollment and graduation. Indeed, despite the controversy surrounding standardized testing, the practice of administering such tests is on the rise. One important reason for this trend is a growing concern with the quality of education in the United States. In 1983 the National Commission on Excellence in Education issued "A Nation at Risk," a well-publicized indictment of this nation's public-school system. Its proclamation that American schools were failing to prepare future generations for the challenges wrought by an increasingly complex society and the needs of the economy and the business world sent a chill through policymakers and shook loose millions of dollars in new state funds for education.

How Will My Child Be Tested?

Testing traditionally begins in a child's first year of primary school and continues throughout her academic career. Standardized tests are also available for even younger children, but most experts don't recommend using them as a sole criteria because the results are often unreliable.

Standardized exams are generally prepared by specialized publishers for national distribution and administered in an identical way—sometimes in a group, other times individually—so that results can be compared within a classroom, across school districts, and from one state to another. Children who are too young to read and write are tested orally, while older children are given written tests. Usually the tests are timed in order to evaluate the ease with which a child performs given tasks.

Most standardized tests can be divided into two broad categories—aptitude tests (I.Q. tests), which measure the capacity to learn, and achievement tests, which measure acquired knowledge. Both are given to primary-grade children, who are most commonly tested on mathematical and reading abilities. Language, motor function, interpersonal abilities, and perceptual and reasoning skills are also frequent test areas.

Can Intelligence Be Measured? A Look at the I.Q. Test

The Intelligence Quotient Test, referred to as the I.Q. test, is certainly the most common—and probably the least understood—of the educational tests administered to primary-school students. When French psychologist Alfred Binet introduced the first such test to the crowded schools of Paris in 1905, his intention was to identify youngsters who would find it difficult to blossom in a regular classroom.

Binet's measurements proved startlingly accurate, and over the years his approach was refined to create the I.Q. test now in widespread use. The Wechsler Intelligence Scale for Children-Revised (WISC-R), the Wechsler Preschool and Primary Scale of Intelligence (WPPSI), and the Stanford-Binet Intelligence Scale are three of the most common forms of the I.Q. test, although there are others as well.

In a typical I.Q. test, a five-year-old child might be asked to complete a puzzle within a certain time period, to answer vocabulary questions, to identify differences and similarities between objects, and to demonstrate an understanding of categories by answering a question such as, ''Is a rose a flower, a tree, or a vegetable?'' Scores follow a bell-shaped curve, with 100 representing the average of all test takers. At the low end of the scale are scores below 70, which indicate developmental disabilities; at the opposite end of the spectrum are scores above 130, which represent what are ''very superior'' intellects. In the United States, 95 percent of all test takers score within the normal range of 70 to 130, 2.5 percent score below 70 and 2.5 percent score above 130.

Contrary to popular assumptions, however, the I.Q. test does not really attempt to reduce the complex and multifaceted nature of human intelligence to a single number. What it does try to do is to predict—in the most general terms—how well a child can be expected to perform in school. Even at that, however, I.Q. test results have severe limitations, and there is a great deal of controversy over their extensive use.

I. Q. test questions have also been harshly criticized for being culturally and economically biased in favor of the white middle class. Passages to test reading comprehension, for example, may describe worlds entirely unfamiliar to poor youngsters of the inner city. Rarely are these children tested on items that would be familiar to them but not to their suburban, middle-class counterparts.

The tests don't tell a complete story because intellectual motivation, personal drive, and family life all have an enormous, but not really measureable, impact on academic achievement. Studies have also shown that I.Q. scores have little connection to an individual's success later in life. Practical intelligence, emotional maturity, and the capacity to deal with disappointment are ultimately more meaningful than the raw number of an I.Q. test, according to the experts. By the same token, a poor test taker may have the positive outlook, sense of self-worth, and other skills of ''constructive thinking'' that contribute to a lifetime of accomplishment.

Achievement Tests

Unlike I.Q. tests, achievement tests are meant to inform teachers and students of how much knowledge of particular subject areas—usually language and mathematics—students have acquired. Properly administered and carefully interpreted, these tests can provide teachers with greater insight into the individual characteristics of their pupils and permit school districts to measure their success relative to others.

At their best, these tests allow educators to:

- Identify children who are having difficulties learning so that remedial action can be taken before they begin to lag behind their classmates.

- Identify intellectually gifted children in order to provide them with additional challenges.

- Begin to assemble a composite picture of a student's achievements and abilities. A stack of test results accumulated over many years of schooling provides much more information than a single score.

It should be noted, however, that observant teachers can compile much of the same information—and often a lot more—based on their daily classroom experience. More significantly, tests that are not properly interpreted can work against a student. Low scores can color the way teachers, parents, and even the child herself views her capacities. A child who is labeled an "underachiever" may feel powerless to improve her performance; thus, the label becomes a self-fulfilling prophecy.

Conversely, someone who is ranked above her peers on standardized tests may be unfairly criticized if her classroom performance doesn't match her test scores. Rather than probing for the real reason a child is struggling through the third grade, for example, her teacher might simply assume she isn't trying hard enough.

Another problem with unduly emphasizing standardized test results is that teachers may be pressured by parents, the taxpaying public, or the school board to "teach to the test." When good teaching is measured strictly by high test scores, a teacher's incentive may be to design a curriculum that creates good test takers rather than to create an environment designed to stimulate independent thinking.

Nor do standardized tests readily reflect certain strengths, although they can work against children with certain weaknesses. Multiple-choice tests, for example, are easy to score, but the results are rather shallow since they allow no room for interpretation or ambiguity. Timed tests usually reward quick thinkers, not creative ones. And a restless child who learns best by doing may be unable to sit still long enough to answer a battery of test questions.

As a parent, you are entitled to know exactly which tests are required in your child's school and just what is done with the results. Almost every state allows you access to your child's school records and test scores, and you should exercise your right to review her files regularly. Critical decisions that may have an impact on a child's future should never be made on the basis of a single score. If a particular test result is markedly lower than your child's norm, or you have any *real* reason to think a score was skewed—perhaps because your child was feeling particularly pressured or ill that day—you may be able to arrange for retesting.

Can Parents Prepare Children for Standardized Tests?

Before your child is tested formally for the first time, you might want to think about your hopes and expectations of her. Psychologically speaking, are you heavily invested in her test scores? If your expectations are unrealistically high, you may be setting yourself up for disappointment—and you may be instilling an unnecessary sense of dread in your child.

You'll both be much better off if you can relax. Instead of focusing on her scores, consider how you can improve your child's test-taking ability. Start by talking to her about the art and science of the test. Explain, in a way that makes sense to her, why tests are given and what will be expected of her in the testing room. Let her know that tests should be taken seriously, but don't overplay their significance.

On the day of the test, see that your child is well-rested, has eaten breakfast, and is well-prepared so that she can perform up to capacity. And when the results are in, be sure to praise her efforts, no matter what the score.

CHAPTER ELEVEN

• • • • • •

Different Children, Different Gifts

Gifts come in many shapes and sizes, and the wrapping can be as varied as the contents. A "gifted" child may be a math whiz or have musical talent, athletic ability, or a knack for making friends.

Although researchers recognize that talents come in many forms and cannot be assessed by any single means, the special in-school "gifted and talented" programs are geared to children with certain *measurable* abilities—in particular, high I.Q. scores, logical thinking abilities, and verbal, often academically oriented, skills. Such programs provide a real advantage to academically talented children, but they don't always take into account the broad spectrum of talents with which children are endowed. Nor does the traditional educational system necessarily recognize, reward, or nurture nontraditional gifts. But as a parent, you can.

According to Dr. Howard Gardner, a researcher at the Harvard Graduate School of Education, we should expand the definitions of the words *creativity* and *intelligence*. "Verbal and mathematical abilities have been put on a pedestal," he says. "People are creative in different areas. There's a strong creative spark in all normal children though it may be expressed in different media. While we are willing to support this early in life, we may inadvertantly snuff out a particular type of intelligence or creativity as children mature."

Who Is Gifted?

Every child is "gifted," and there are many special traits that often go unrecognized, including persistence, enthusiasm, caution, courage, generosity, stamina, imagination, inquisitiveness, and flexibility.

David, for instance, is enthusiastic about whatever he does—so much so that he has a hard time waiting his turn—and he's ahead of his playmates in some school-related skills. Emily, on the other hand, steps back to watch and analyze before getting involved in an activity. She waits to participate until she's confident she can accomplish the task. Clearly, each child has a unique personality and unique gifts.

Research with infants has demonstrated that even newborns have particular personality traits, many of which last into childhood. Persistence and reaction to new situations are among the characteristics exhibited early on. However, life experience helps determine which personality traits blossom and which ones don't. How parents view and respond to these traits plays a key role in how a child develops.

Of course, personal characteristics can be viewed either positively or negatively. Katie is extremely determined about learning new things. When she wants to try to ride her two-wheeler down the driveway one more time, it takes all of her mother's patience not to call her *stubborn* instead of *persistent*. Eric, on the other hand, is very sensitive toward other children's feelings. While his father worries that he's not assertive enough, his teacher recognizes him as exceptionally thoughtful and considerate.

Gifts can also have many different components: Athletic skill may be a function of agility, speed, strength, perseverance, or cooperativeness. The child with musical talent may have a great sense of rhythm, perfect pitch, exuberance, or imagination.

How Do I Identify My Child's Gifts?

One of the most important gifts you can give to your child is an appreciation of his uniqueness, of what he *alone* brings into the world. Doing that sometimes involves examining the relationship between your values and your child's personality and setting aside your own notions of what makes a child special.

- **Appreciate individuality.** Because of the powerful effect you have on your child, you need to look closely at what you value and how that affects the talents you're encouraging. When parents' and children's interests mesh, it's easy to support a talent. But when what you like differs from what your child likes, you may have to make a special effort to share his enthusiasm.

  Since adult expectations can influence how children view themselves, it is important for you to recognize your child's *strengths.* Building on strengths is an effective way to help your child develop not just skills but self-esteem as well. Recognizing what your child enjoys doing and is "good at" is an extremely important first step. Then you can support and encourage those abilities—without pushing.

- **Observe your child.** Children behave differently in different settings and with different people. One child may be talkative with adults but shy with other children. Another may have boundless energy in the backyard but have trouble sitting still for any length of time.

  Noticing how each child is special, how he reacts with adults or with other kids, and how he plays alone, helps clue parents in on their child's special talents.

  Listening carefully to what your child says is important, too. Does he express a concern for animals? An interest in adventure? A whimsical sense of humor? Watch his body language. Is he precise and meticulous? Or does he fly around the house like one of his superheroes? What captures his attention? Is it the ant crawling along the sidewalk? The fire engine zooming by? The next-door neighbor describing his conversation in the shoe store? What does your child learn to do quickly and enthusiastically? Ride a bike? Play the xylophone? Recognize the makes of cars? By getting to know him as a real individual, you'll be able to recognize what is unique and special about him.

- **Share activities.** Chances are that there are some activities you and your child do share an interest in. Maybe you both enjoy doing puzzles, cooking, or telling jokes. Find those activities and build on them. Create special times to work on things together. If there are other skills and interests you don't share, you might find a relative or friend who can act as a role model. Studies have shown that role models play a large part in encouraging kids to pursue and develop their abilities. Tracing the childhoods of several accomplished adults, educator Benjamin Bloom of the University of Chicago found that these children's earliest mentors were generally nurturing and enthusiastic but were not necessarily skilled experts.

- **Support interests.** If your child loves the inside of a motor and you don't know the difference between a spark plug and a muffler, try visiting a local auto-repair shop for a look around. Most adults are happy to talk to children who appreciate what they're doing, especially if you let them know in advance and plan for a quiet moment. Similarly, collecting dinosaur models may not be exciting to you, but your child may find it fascinating. Ask your child what he likes about *Tyrannosaurus rex*. And recognize that although most preschool dinosaur lovers don't grow up to be paleontologists, some do. Let your child know that such grown-ups exist. If your child is in school, share what you know about his interests with the teacher, who can help develop them further.

- **Enrich your child's environment.** In addition to role models, there are other resources that can support a child's gifts. Locate books, magazines, and toys that encourage a special interest or ability. You can also provide your child with a rich environment by going on trips to the zoo, the park, concerts, the library, and the local museum. Expose him to many different places and activities. In most communities, it is possible to find lessons geared specifically to children in music, gymnastics, or other skills.

- **Take it easy.** Just be on guard not to push. It is more important for young children to maintain their enjoyment of an activity than to learn complex skills. Children who are pushed beyond their enthusiasm may lose interest entirely. Always let the activity remain the child's. If he asks the difference between a maple and an oak, it's not necessary to dash to the library for a dozen books on botany. Let your child set the pace, but do take an active part in supporting his interests.

- **Leave room for change.** While children may show strong interests and skills in one area, it is important not to label Sara as the artist, Brian as the mathematician, or Jeannie as the future doctor in a way that limits their opportunities to explore other areas. Children are always in a fluid state, and what appeals to them today may not tomorrow. They change and develop new abilities over time. Take the cues from your child.

A child's special gifts can be a source of pleasure and self-esteem. If you help your child discover what he loves and is good at, if you encourage his talents and support his endeavors, you will help him fulfill his unique potential.

What About Intellectually Gifted Kids?

Some children are brighter than others—and some are *much* brighter. This wide divergence of abilities is a reality that must be dealt with.

Many people assume that highly intelligent children will fare well in any classroom. The truth is that they frequently do not. Some gifted children, bored and frustrated, develop behavior problems and may even become dropouts. Teachers are often put off by the challenges of teaching very bright students. Many bright students end up working far below their potential. Parents see these strains on their children, and they worry.

Advocates for the gifted child also come up against the fear that if the schools provide special programs for these children, other children will be slighted. This fear is largely unjustified, say most educators. For one thing, many of the changes sought by parents of gifted children would benefit *all* children. A learning environment where differences in abilities and interests are taken into account helps all children work up to their potential. Parents can work together to upgrade the schools in these directions, and everyone will come out ahead.

The Preschool Years

The school years present tough problems for gifted children and their parents. It seems a little easier for parents of precocious preschoolers, but some concerns have already reared their heads. Should the child be in a special preschool program? Should parents do a lot of teaching on their own? Are there "educational toys" or materials that should be bought?

Experts on gifted children say that the best policy is for parents to follow their child's own interests, lending support where they can. This is good advice for *any* parent, as a matter of fact. For example, if your son is interested in snakes this month, take him to the reptile room at the zoo. Encourage him to talk to the librarian about what he'd like to find out about snakes. But be cautious—such parental "support" can be overdone. Don't drag your child into heavy reptilian research. Just help out by making resources and experiences available. It's especially useful to show him how he can find out more about things he's interested in. Then allow him to pursue his interest as far as it takes him.

For parents of gifted children, another issue that begins in the preschool years is the matter of playmates. Parents of one intellectually gifted boy report the struggles of their son Jay, who at age four was already reading *Newsweek* and writing his own comic strips. His mother says, "With the kids Jay's age, one of two things happened. Either Jay dominated the other child with all his ideas and verbal skills—'Let's do this . . . Now you do that'—or else they just didn't connect at all, neither one understanding what the other was doing. When he tried to play with the older kids, he was just a little kid to them. They had no more use for him than for any other four-year-old."

This is a common situation for the gifted child. Playing with someone who is more or less an equal (physically, socially, intellectually) is a special kind of experience in learning to work together and to get along. And for people of any age it is a special kind of pleasure. Adults and older children can seek out people with whom they have a lot in common. Young children can't do this. So, though the gifted child benefits from all kinds of playmates, he will enjoy the opportunity to play regularly with a friend or two who share his interests and ability level. (See the "Resources" section at the back of this book for a list of organizations that help parents of gifted children find each other, both for the purposes of getting children together and for the chance to talk about their shared concerns.)

The Best Gift: A Realistic and Positive Self-Image

For any child, there will always be someone who is smarter than he is—or more athletic, or whatever. No individual will always be the best at everything. If you don't want your child to be resentful of, or intimidated by, the superior talents of others, you must watch out for the messages you are sending. Avoid making comments that belittle or begrudge the contributions and talents of other people—adults or children. Take care not to place too much value on being smartest or best, lest your child begin to place his whole sense of worth on where he stands intellectually.

Regardless of what you do, there are going to be times when your child will be upset because someone else's abilities or achievements are more outstanding than his own. A person's self-esteem is on a firm foundation when it is linked to qualities like persistence, thoughtfulness in approaching problems, and flexibility in tackling tasks. Perhaps the best antidote of all to resentment of our limitations is a sense of humor. These are the kinds of qualities that every child can develop, and they are the sound basis for a self-image that is positive and realistic. With such a self-image, any child will be able to enjoy to the fullest his own special abilities and talents.

What About the Learning-Disabled Child?

There are a number of reasons why some children have difficulty learning, and since children develop according to individual timetables, determining that a particular child is not progressing as he should be is not always easy.

If parents are concerned about whether or not a child is developing at roughly the same pace as his peers, they should first look for physical or emotional causes for any apparent lag in development. Hearing or vision problems, for instance, can prevent a child from absorbing the information he needs if he is to learn. Poor nutrition, too, can leave a child unable to concentrate. Chronic emotional problems, as well as temporary emotional upsets, disrupt the learning process. Children with low self-esteem often lack the motivation to learn. A child whose ability to learn is hampered by physical or emotional problems is not necessarily learning-disabled. Conversely, poor eyesight or hearing or emotional problems do not cause learning disabilities. Therefore, before a child who is having difficulty learning is diagnosed as having a learning disability, it's essential that these possible causes for his difficulties are addressed.

What Is a Learning Disability?

Most experts agree that a learning disability is a condition that prevents a child from reaching his full potential because his brain fails to process the information it receives. Some children, although their hearing and eyesight are normal, are unable to understand what they hear or see. Words or images simply do not make sense to them. Other children can process spoken language but cannot interpret written symbols, such as letters and numbers. These problems are called *perceptual disabilities.* According to the American Academy of Pediatrics, the problem that learning-disabled children experience "is similar to a distorted television picture caused by 'technical problems' at the station. There is nothing wrong with the TV camera at the station or the TV set in your home. Yet, the picture is not clear. Something in the internal workings of the TV station prevents it from presenting a good picture." In other words, they say, "The problem occurs in the brain *after* the eyes and ears have done their job."

What Causes Learning Disabilities and How Can They Be Detected?

There is evidence that learning disabilities run in families, and parents who had difficulties in school or whose siblings had difficulties should be particularly alert for signs of learning disabilities in their children. Heredity is not the only risk factor. Children who experience stress during or soon after birth can develop problems, as can children who are born too small. Physical traumas, such as cancer treatment, infections of the central nervous system, or severe head injuries, can also increase a child's risk of developing a learning disability. In other cases, the causes of a learning disability cannot be determined.

The earlier a child with a learning disability is diagnosed, the earlier treatment can begin. A child who is diagnosed and treated early is less likely to suffer from the emotional problems, such as depression or withdrawal, that often accompany his disability. Parents of preschoolers should consider the following factors, while keeping in mind that these warning signs do not always indicate a learning disability.

- **Delayed language development.** By age two-and-a-half, a child should be able to create short sentences. By age three, his speech should be understandable at least half of the time.

- **Poor coordination.** By age five, a child should be able to hop on one foot, use scissors correctly, button his clothes, and put on his shoes.

- **Short attention span.** By age four, a child should be able to concentrate long enough to be read to or to complete a simple puzzle or other activity, and to follow simple directions.

It is also important to note that these are not the only signs to look for. If you have concerns, even though your child displays none of these symptoms, it is important to consult a professional.

What Kinds of Treatment Are Available?

While there are no cures for learning disabilities, learning-disabled children *can* learn and *can* reach their potentials in spite of their disabilities, provided that they receive the proper treatment in a supportive atmosphere.

Most local school districts are able to arrange for testing to determine *if* a disability exists. Under the Education for all Handicapped Children Act (PL 94–142), signed into law in November of 1975, federal funds are available for all children with special needs. That legislation requires school systems to provide free evaluation of school-age youngsters suspected of being learning-disabled. Sometimes screening is available for preschoolers, too; if not, school-district staff can refer you to a community screening program or to a private consultant.

A thorough evaluation includes a battery of tests, usually administered by a team of educational and psychological professionals to rule out any physical problems. Once testing is complete, parents should receive an in-depth briefing on the findings and be provided with appropriate service referrals. For a school-age child, the school district is required to draft an Individual Education Plan (IEP) to be presented and discussed with the parents, which details a child's abilities and weaknesses and sets behavioral and learning goals that are revised every year. PL 94–172 declares that all children with physical or learning disabilities are entitled to appropriate education in the "least restrictive" environment possible. Many learning-disabled children thus remain in regular classrooms while receiving extra remedial attention; others, however, may learn best if they are enrolled in separate special-education classes.

Sometimes the issue of holding a child back—grade retention—is raised with learning-disabled youngsters. As with gifted children, the decision is tied to both a child's intellectual achievements and his level of social skills and emotional development. A host of factors need to be considered, but a sound argument can be made for allowing a child who is lagging socially as well as academically to repeat a grade. On the other hand, a youngster who is behind in just one subject area or has a lot of friends in his class may be better served by receiving the individualized instruction he needs to be promoted.

How Can Parents Help Their Children Cope?

Helping your child cope with his difficulty in learning and maximizing his strengths to the greatest extent possible means educating yourself about his disabilities and talking openly with him about his problems. You can also take some of these steps to help him cope:

- **Notice his efforts and praise them.** Show him that you are pleased when he is successful, no matter how small the achievement. Help him to value persistence and to achieve a sense of power over his environment by setting small and realistic goals that he can meet.

- **Never convey a sense of disappointment with your child's limitations** and don't expect more of him than he can give. Don't interfere when he is trying to do something for himself or he may feel he is not competent to do it.

- **Help him develop language skills.** Verbal skills are a frequent source of problems for a child with learning disabilities. To help improve his facility with language, talk frequently to him, encourage him to speak, respond directly to what he is saying, and bolster his vocabulary with words that describe your activities. While working to improve your child's ability to communicate, accept pantomime and hand gestures as a valid form of language. When giving instructions to your child, speak clearly, be precise, and repeat them as many times as necessary. You may also want your child to repeat important instructions back to you to be certain he grasps what you are saying and can remember it.

- **Discipline appropriately.** Discipline is a particular problem with some learning-disabled children because their parents have to distinguish between behavior that is deliberately disobedient and that which the child is powerless to change. Never punish your child for things he has no control over. By the same token, don't allow him to take advantage of you. Consistently applied and appropriate discipline is important for all children.

- **Use the skills a child has developed in one arena to improve his skills elsewhere.** If arithmetic is his downfall but he loves to cook, ask him to help you double a recipe. If he'd rather be traipsing through the woods than studying, combine a nature walk with a lesson on the plants and animals of the forest. Build up reading skills by selecting books on subjects that interest him.

- **Build his self-esteem.** Bolstering a child's self-esteem by emphasizing his strengths is critical. If he is having trouble with science, for example, help but don't relentlessly drill him on the subject. Instead, tell him, ''I know it's frustrating not to understand the lessons as well as the other kids, but your teacher says you are one of the best artists in your class.''

- **Establish routines.** Because they have reason to mistrust their own judgments, learning-disabled children are most comfortable in stable, predictable situations and may become extremely upset when familiar patterns are broken. Whenever possible, maintain habitual routines and make sure your child knows what's expected of him.

Whether he is learning-disabled or not, the child who can take setbacks in stride, rather than seeing them as a reflection of his self-worth, is one who is well equipped to cope with life's frustrations, challenges, and opportunities. By helping a child accept and compensate for his learning disability, parents play a crucial role in a healthy adjustment process.

CHAPTER TWELVE

• • • • • •

How to Help Your Child Succeed in School

Just about every educational theorist and hands-on prac-
titioner agrees that a solid partnership between parents
and the school district is the key to effective education. All
evidence suggests that in an atmosphere of cooperation,
student motivation jumps, academic achievement soars,
and the relationship between the school and the community improves significantly. As educators Tom and Harriet
Sobol explain in *Your Child in School*: "When the school
reflects the values of the home and the home supports the
efforts of the school, children grow in an atmosphere of
shared purposes and consistent expectations. There is no
room for confusion about what is important. . . . Attaining
this unity of purpose requires effective communication between home and school."

How can you form a good parent-teacher partnership that
will benefit your child? The first step is getting to know
your child's teacher.

The Parent-Teacher Relationship

Caring and effective primary-school teachers often develop strong bonds with their young pupils and forge equally close working relationships with the parents of those pupils. The ideal parent-teacher partnership is predicated on the notion that the partners share a single goal: meeting the best interests of a child. Once they trust and respect one another, parents and teachers can meet regularly to exchange insights and observations. And if either party disagrees with an approach taken by the other, each one should be able to explain why, in a candid and constructive manner.

Admittedly, establishing such a relationship requires commitment and hard work. In a classroom of some twenty or thirty children, a teacher may mistakenly interpret parental inquiries and suggestions as outside interference— and no one wants to be told how to do her job. Conversely, parents may be tempted to abdicate all responsibility by laying the burden of a child's education entirely on the school's doorstep. But these problems can be overcome when the lines of communication between parents and teachers are kept open. Classroom conferences are one of the best places in which to build and maintain a healthy partnership.

How to Talk to Your Child's Teacher

Before each school year ends, parents everywhere open the door to their child's classroom, squeeze themselves into an undersize chair, and settle down for a parent-teacher conference. Some look forward to these occasions. Others dread them. Whatever your feeling, a few basic rules of communication can ensure that school conferences become not only pleasant but also helpful and informative. To make the most of parent-teacher conferences:

- **Prepare ahead.** It helps if you have a list of things you would like to talk about. Parent-teacher conferences are short, and it makes good sense not to have to use the first five minutes to collect your thoughts.

  Base your list of topics for discussion on the observations you've made over the course of the school term. Before the conference, ask your child if there is anything she would like you to talk about with the teacher. Among the usual requests for less homework and more playtime, you might get some important messages, such as her desire to be moved to a different spot for a better view of the chalkboard.

- **Try to be objective.** Sitting in one of those tiny chairs, it is easy to feel like a child again and to view your offspring's triumphs and defeats as your own. It is difficult, but essential, to remember that school is your child's responsibility. Recognizing this fact will allow you to maintain an objective outlook and to cooperate with the teacher in helping your child profit from school.

- **Speak concretely and constructively.** To be sure of getting your points across to the teacher, phrase your concerns as concretely as possible and give examples that show what you mean. "Chris is having a terrible time with homework" doesn't tell the teacher very much. But if you say that Chris struggles with her spelling assignment and stayed up past her bedtime three times last week—and *still* couldn't get it finished—the picture becomes much clearer.

  Speak your mind and voice your feelings, but make sure you state them as just that—personal feelings or opinions—rather than as statements of fact. "You put too much emphasis on handwriting in your class" may or may not be true, but it is certainly true that such a pronouncement will alienate all but the toughest-skinned instructor. It's okay, however, to say, "I feel that handwriting is being given too much importance." No one can quarrel with that—you have merely given your opinion.

When you want to disagree with the teacher's way of handling a situation, phrase your opinion in a constructive manner. "I believe that Jenny works harder if she knows exactly what is expected of her" will probably bring better results than "You never let the kids know what they're supposed to be doing."

Don't be afraid to make requests and suggest alternatives: "Alice has been telling me lately that she gets bored in reading class. Perhaps you could suggest some extra reading for her when she's finished with the assignment." And voice your child's desires—to be called on more often, to be given a chance to shake out the erasers—if they seem reasonable.

- **Listen carefully.** Have your say with the teacher. Tell her what you're pleased with and what you're worried about. And then, *listen.* Don't prejudge the teacher or assume that you know what she's going to say. Remember, teachers see a very different side of your child than you do. While you may not agree with all aspects of the teacher's educational philosophy, she lives in that classroom with many children every day.

- **Share with your child.** After the conference, share the results with your child. Be sure to mention any positive remarks the teacher made about the child's performance, and try to maintain an objective attitude about the others. Your goal should be to impart useful information ("Ms. Jones thinks that it is important for you to prepare for your spelling tests'') rather than to heap blame (''If you weren't so lazy, you'd get better grades in spelling'').

Ask your child what she thinks she can do to improve her work. A first-grader who comes up with the idea that she should gather her school things the night before to avoid leaving important papers at home is well on her way to becoming a responsible student.

Parent-teacher conferences are opportunities for communication for all involved. The time you spend squeezed into that miniature chair can have a powerful impact on your child's schooling. It is worth preparing for and using fully—and you may even learn to enjoy it.

Homework

Most research suggests that formal homework assignments are ineffective for very young children and should be used sparingly. By the third grade, however, children are usually ready to be completing homework regularly. When the assignments are appropriate to a child's learning level and parents show genuine interest in them, homework can serve a number of productive purposes.

What Works: Research About Teaching and Learning, a report of the U.S. Department of Education issued in 1986, states the following: ''Student achievement rises significantly when teachers regularly assign homework and students conscientiously do it. . . . Effective homework assignments do not just supplement the classroom lesson; they also teach students to be independent learners. Homework gives students experience in following directions, making judgments and comparisons, raising additional questions for study, and developing responsibility and self-discipline.''

Homework can also foster the development of good study habits, reinforce the day's lessons, and give children an opportunity to practice skills they have been studying in the classroom. Appropriate assignments encourage children to think creatively and to take initiative. The work need not be time-consuming to be effective. Having a child bring in a snapshot from home and tell a story about it, for example, is both a lesson in doing research and a tool to stimulate the imagination.

Homework is one important way that parents can stay informed about their child's activities in school, and it can strengthen the bond between the home and the classroom. To make the most of the child's homework experience, parents can and should be involved. For example:

- **Be certain that the child participates in setting the ground rules for getting her homework done.** Obviously, you've got to limit her options—not doing homework at all isn't a choice, for example—but you could certainly discuss when and where she prefers to study and find out if she'd rather review her assignments with you as she goes along or after they are all completed.

- **Furnish your child with a work space of her own**—a small desk or even a corner of a table is fine if it provides privacy and encourages a sense of pride and ownership.

- **When you ask your child about the tasks she needs to complete, be sure to communicate the fact that you really care about what she is learning,** rather than suggesting in any way that you don't trust her to complete her assignments without interference.

- **Often it is best to let a child romp and play right after school before helping her settle down to homework.** Perhaps you and your child will agree that assigned tasks need to be completed before dinner or before watching television. Whatever works best for all concerned is fine as long as the rules are clear and consistently enforced. Once homework becomes a routine part of your child's day, she will be less likely to neglect it and you will be more able to act as a facilitator, not an enforcer.

- **Offer help as needed.** Here, you will have to find a comfortable balance between two extremes: unnecessary interference and insufficient attention. Setting aside a specific time slot every evening to discuss schoolwork clearly communicates the value you assign it. During each evening's session, you can review your child's assignments, provide some tutoring assistance if necessary, or just talk about her day at school.

- **Resist the temptation to take over a youngster's assignments.** Children need space to learn from their errors and to try to correct them on their own. This doesn't mean, however, that every question brought to you should be handed back to the child. Instead, you could offer to join her in looking up the answer.

What can be done about the child who just doesn't complete her homework assignments? A parent's first task is to find out why, and it is best to start at the source: Have a nonconfrontational talk with your child, explain your concerns, and get her involved in finding a solution to the problem. Be certain that she understands what is expected of her and that she has the necessary resources to meet those expectations. A parent-teacher conference might be in order if the child seems repeatedly confused about what she is supposed to do.

You may also want to create rules about television watching and after-school activities and be certain that her working conditions are conducive to study. Once you have done what you can to encourage your child to complete her assignments, leave the responsibility to her and let her face the consequences of failing to get the work done. (This strategy works only if the child dislikes the consequences and takes steps to correct herself.) If she continuously rejects taking responsibility for her schoolwork, the problem is likely larger than her relationship with school, and you may want to seek professional help in overcoming her resistance.

Afterword:
Putting It All Together
• • • • • •

The Parents Young Learners Need

Children, as we've seen, think differently than adults. They process information differently. They look for meaning in information an adult might ignore—like the repetition of a question. They pay attention to some things adults take for granted, and they have little patience for some details adults find fascinating.

As we've seen, child-development experts try to define exactly how the world looks to children. But the broadly stated stages and the landmarks listed on development charts are of limited help to an adult who has just a few kids to care for. In real life, change is gradual. The landmarks don't always come in sequence. Even less often do they meet a textbook's timetable.

The world doesn't just look different to "children." It looks different to *each* child, because each child is different—physically, intellectually, in interests, in attitudes, in values, in temperament. Not only that, but to each child, the world looks different each day. That's what growing up is about: continually changing and changing our understanding of the world we live in.

Kids change for all the reasons we've considered: physical development of muscles, bones, and brains; the unfolding of plans encoded in their genes; and the new experiences they encounter daily. Kids learn as they change, and they change as they learn. They develop tastes and opinions, learning tactics, problem-solving styles, and ways of understanding their culture—whether they meet that culture in other people's attitudes, at play, or in school.

There's no recipe for raising children. Across time and history, kids have grown up in small families and in large ones. They've been cared for by parents, grandparents, sisters and brothers, nannies, nursemaids, and carefully trained child-care professionals. They've spent their days in farms and fields, in city playgrounds and suburban backyards. They've had caretakers who were permissive and caretakers who were strict. They've grown up in diverse cultures, in many varied ways.

But no matter what the culture, no matter what the style of upbringing, kids have grown up. By and large, they've grown up to be perfectly decent adults—a generation at least as good as their parents.

All those grown-up "kids" have learned, too—at every step of the way. Kids learn their whole childhoods long. They learn from the flowers they smell. They learn from the mushiness of the pillows they lay their heads on each night. They learn from the flavors of breakfast in the morning, from the shows on TV, and from the family cat. Most of all, they learn from people—primarily from their parents.

Parents don't have total control over a child's learning environment, especially as the child gets older, but their influence can help shape the world in which and from which their children learn.

To provide the best educational opportunities for their children, parents don't need to turn themselves into formal schoolteachers. Likewise, children needn't be trained for school the way athletes are trained for the Olympics. There is no proven advantage to learning to read, write, or water-ski by age four. Preschoolers have more than enough to learn from their world without the stress and structure of formal instruction.

As a parent, you just need to be a guide. It can help to think of your child as a guest and a companion on a voyage through a world you know well but that he's seeing for the first time. It's a world with its own customs and manners, its own foods and artistic styles, even its own laws of physics. Your companion is going to want to try a lot of things out (and to skip a few that you know are good for him!). He's going to need a good deal of explanation. He's going to need attention. And you're going to have to put yourself in his place, to imagine the world as he experiences it and to explain it in terms he'll understand.

Before long, your companion is going to go off by himself, have a few experiences, and come back to you. You'll help him more if you take his experiences into account, if you respect the interests he's developing, if you give him credit for what he's learned. Sometimes he'll say things that seem to make no sense, or he'll act in ways that seem inappropriate. You'll help most if you try to understand your companion's point of view.

The Needs of Young Learners

There are, of course, a few needs parents can meet. Good nutrition is one, since the process of learning rests so much on the physical base of the nervous system. Varied experience helps, too. Children don't need specially designed learning experiences. They just need the normal experiences of daily life: playing, sharing meals, taking a trip to the grocery store, doing chores, hearing a story at bedtime.

Plain old everyday talking is a good example of a normal, spontaneous learning experience. Even the youngest children benefit when adults talk with them. They learn the sounds of language; they feel the attention and emotion directed their way. They become comfortable about being included in social situations. As they grow older, children build vocabulary and learn the structure of language—all through chatting.

Children need physical challenges as well. Playing with simple toys, building with blocks, climbing stairs, fashioning sand castles, splashing in the bath or a pool all help children learn about the physical world while they help strengthen and coordinate young muscles. As children become more capable physically, they enjoy and learn from using adult tools and equipment: brooms, shovels, hammers, pencils, and so forth.

Above all, children need encouragement. They need parents who support their natural curiosity, who enable them to explore the world safely, to test their ideas in fantasy play, to indulge in a little rough-and-tumble fun. If the environment is interesting and supportive, kids will take care of the learning themselves.

The Parents' Role

All parents reach limits from time to time; we yell a little, spend a little more time on our own needs than perhaps we should. We don't have the money to buy things we wish our children could have. Sometimes we forget that the child we're dealing with is just that—a child.

Luckily, children don't need perfection. What they need is caring and respect. They need parents who listen—even when the children aren't speaking in words. They need parents who pay attention to their feelings and try to imagine the way their children see the world. They need parents who understand that language is a tool that children are just learning to use and who take that into account in conversation.

When the parents have something important to say—an instruction, a bit of information, a warning—or when they're simply chatting, they try to speak in words and sentences that make sense to the child. They try not to assume that kids understand grown-up language.

The parents try to support their kids' efforts to learn about the world. They take a moment to explain what they're doing, whether baking a pie, changing a tire, or programming a VCR. They keep an eye out for their children's interests and try to extend their opportunities in these areas. But when they find out they were wrong, or that they pushed too hard too fast, they take it in stride. They recognize that kids need time off, too. Sometimes the best times kids have, the times they think and learn the most, are the times when they're doing "nothing."

Children need parents who let them know that they're loved. When they praise, and when they criticize, they speak about specifics—a good throw, a bossy remark to a younger sibling. They try not to write their kids off with a label—artistic, brilliant, good, clumsy, stupid, or bratty.

Children need parents who know that they never know what a kid may do—or say—next. They know that children change, and they welcome the changes. They give a child room to make mistakes and to learn from his mistakes himself. They let him know he won't lose face by trying something new and failing. They try to let their children feel safe trying again.

Children need parents who recognize that they're not raising kids by themselves. Like it or not, the entire world is chipping in, and so are the genes inside each child's body. These parents make choices—limits on TV or comic books, plenty of vegetables at dinner, no wearing torn dungarees to school—but they respect children's reactions and opinions. They understand it's sometimes hard for mere parents to get their way.

All parents make mistakes, but children need parents who try to acknowledge theirs. They're not afraid to tell a child, "I messed up." They're not afraid to give a reason their child will understand. Nor are they afraid, from time to time, to say, "Because I said so."

Children need parents who try to be the kind of people they'd like their kids to be. Most of all, they need parents who recognize that they're learning, too. They're learning about this remarkable individual, this young person with a mind, a body, and a destiny all his own.

In any bookstore or library, you'll find shelves and shelves of books promising to teach you about children. Like this book, many of them may hold genuine help. But no expert anywhere has written a book about *your* kid—or your next kid, or your next. Each is different.

Watch your kids. Listen to them. Learn with them. And have a good time.

Resources

••••••

Organizations

General

Children's Art Foundation (CAF), P.O. Box 83, Santa Cruz, CA 95063 (408) 426-5557

The purpose of this organization is to encourage children to develop their literary and artistic potential. CAF sponsors art classes and maintains a 1,000-volume library of children's books and a museum of children's drawings, paintings, and writings.

Publications include *Stone Soup,* a magazine written and illustrated by children.

Gesell Institute of Human Development, 310 Prospect Street, New Haven, CT 06511 (203) 777-3481

Founded by Dr. Arnold Gesell in 1911, this nonprofit research organization deals with child growth and development, child behavior, child psychology, and developmental assessment. It provides clinical services in child development for children up to age fourteen and offers consultations in psychological and developmental evaluation, school readiness, and developmental curriculum.

Home and School Institute (HSI), Special Projects Office, 1201 16th Street, N.W., Room 228, Washington, DC 20036 (202) 466-3633

HSI is concerned with family education for families with children from preschool to junior high. It provides training for family involvement and materials for educating children at home without duplicating the work of the schools.

Services include workshops, curricula, and parent programs for schools, child-abuse-prevention curriculum, and staff/parent workshops for health- and social-service agencies. Books for parents cover home-learning activities for children of varying ages and disabilities. Also available is the *Survival Guide for Busy Parents*, intended to help working parents, single parents, and young parents.

National Association for the Education of Young Children, 1834 Connecticut Avenue, N.W., Washington, DC 20009 (202) 232-8777

This organization provides educational resources for adults who are committed to improving the quality and availability of services for children from birth through age eight. There are more than 60,000 members and 350 local, state, and regional affiliate groups. Their Child Care Information Service provides resource information and referrals of child-care agencies.

Publications include pamphlets and brochures, such as "How to Choose a Good Early Childhood Program," and a journal for members, entitled *Young Children.*

National PTA—National Congress of Parents and Teachers, 700 North Rush, Chicago, IL 60611 (312) 787-0977

This child-advocacy association is dedicated to the health, education, and safety of children and teens. It has more than 26,000 local chapters and 6.4 million members. A national convention for its members is held annually.

Publications include inexpensive booklets and monographs, films, filmstrips, recordings, and posters on many aspects of education, the prize-winning periodical *PTA Today,* and a newsletter, *What's Happening in Washington.*

National Black Child Development Institute, 1463 Rhode Island Avenue, N.W., Washington, DC 20005, (202) 387-1281

This is an advocacy organization dedicated to improving the quality of life for black children. On a national level its efforts focus on child development, child care, child welfare, and education issues. Local affiliates often work on issues that are significant in their geographic areas, such as community development, adoption, foster care, or financial issues.

Publications include a quarterly newsletter, *The Black Child Advocate*, and booklets such as "Guidelines for Adoption Services to Black Families."

National Committee for Citizens in Education (NCEE), 10840 Little Patuxent Parkway, Suite 301, Columbia, MD 21044 (301) 997-9300; (800) 638-9675

The NCEE is a citizen advocacy group for public education devoted to improving the quality of public schools through increased public involvement. NCEE provides the information resources parents and other citizens need to become involved in school decision making at the local level. They also have a program that trains parents and educators to work together constructively.

Services include a computerized clearinghouse of school-related information for parents who call their toll-free hot line, a direct-mail catalog carrying many publications focused on public involvement and school improvement, and a monthly newsletter, *Network*.

Reading Is Fundamental (RIF), 600 Maryland Avenue, S.W., Suite 500, Washington, DC 20024 (202) 287-3220

RIF promotes children's reading through grass-roots projects and a series of publications and workshops for parents. Their purpose is to involve children, from preschool to high school, in reading activities that are aimed at showing that reading is fun. Write to RIF for a brochure of their low-cost publications.

School Age Child Care Project (SACC), Wellesley College, Center for Research on Women, Wellesley, MA 02181 (617) 431-1453

SACC is committed to promoting and enhancing the development of programs and services for children ages five through twelve before and after school and at all times when there is a need for care and supervision.

Publications include the *SACC Newsletter*, which reports on programs nationwide, announces resources and conferences, and reviews books, and a booklet entitled "When School's Out and Nobody's Home." A brochure of publications is available.

Handicapped and Learning-Disabled

Association for Children and Adults with Learning Disabilities (ACLD), 4156 Library Road, Pittsburgh, PA 15234 (412) 341-1515

The national ACLD office provides general information about learning disabilities. The 800 local chapters provide referrals to physicians and treatment centers, and some direct services, such as parent counseling, are provided by many of the chapters.

The resource center at the national headquarters has 500 publications for sale and rents films. Lists of materials are available on request.

Autism Society of America, 1234 Massachusetts Avenue, N.W., Suite 1017, Washington, DC 20005 (202) 783-0125

This national agency is dedicated to the education and welfare of people with autism, as well as those with childhood schizophrenia and other profound behavioral and/or communicative disorders.

Publications include a bimonthly newsletter, *The Advocate*, and booklets such as "How They Grow: A Handbook for Parents of Young Children with Autism."

Clearinghouse on the Handicapped, U.S. Department of Education, Office of Special Education and Rehabilitative Services, Switzer Building, Room 3132, 330 C Street, S.W., Washington, DC 20202-2524 (202) 732-1245

The Clearinghouse provides disability-related information to handicapped individuals, parents, and their service providers. Publications include a seasonal newsletter, *OSER's News in Print*, which details federal activities affecting the handicapped, and a booklet, "A Summary of Existing Legislation Affecting Persons with Disabilities."

Early Childhood Direction Center/Center on Human Policy, New York State Education Department, Division of Program Development, Room 1066, Albany, NY 12234 (518) 474-5804

The Center offers information, support, and referrals for families of young disabled children. Its goal is to promote the integration of persons with disabilities into the mainstream of society. Call for a catalogue of publications.

Council for Exceptional Children— See listing under "Gifted."

International Parents' Organization (IPO), 3417 Volta Place, N.W., Washington, DC 20007 (202) 337-5220

This association of affiliated parents was founded in 1957 within the Alexander Graham Bell Association for the Deaf. Its goal is to give the parents of hearing-impaired children the chance to work together for better conditions for their children through auditory/oral education. IPO provides network and referral services for auditory programs and information on infant screening.

National Information Center for Handicapped Children and Youth, P.O. Box 1492, Washington, DC 20013 (703) 898-6061; toll-free number: 1-800-999-5599

The Center provides free information to assist parents, educators, caregivers, advocates, and others in helping children and youths with disabilities to become participating members of the community.

Publications include free periodic newsletters and other print materials of interest to parents, professionals, advocates, and anyone else concerned with handicapped children and youth.

National Organization of Down's Syndrome/Parents of Down's Syndrome Children (PODSC), c/o Montgomery County Association for Retarded Citizens, 11160 Nebel Street, Rockville, MD 20852 (301) 984-5792; toll-free number: 1-800-232-6372

This organization holds informal meetings and provides parent-to-parent counseling. Additionally, PODSC contacts new parents of Down's Syndrome children to advise them of reading materials, diagnostic tests and clinics, infant-stimulation programs, area schools, recreation programs, and psychological, genetic, and educational counseling.

National Society for Autistic Children, 101 Richmond Street, Huntington, WV 25702 (304) 523-1912

This organization provides an extensive list of publications dealing with autistic and other emotionally handicapped children and publishes case histories—all at no charge. Additionally, the society provides tax information, advice on schools, camps, and hospitals, and information on programs addressed to the needs of autistic children.

Orton Dyslexia Society, 724 York Road, Baltimore, MD 21204 (301) 296-0232; toll-free number: 1-800-ABCD-123

The Orton Dyslexia Society is an international organization for professionals, adult dyslexics, and parents of dyslexic children. It disseminates information related to dyslexia and guides persons with dyslexia and parents of dyslexic children to available resources for diagnosis, remediation, and tutoring. The Society has forty branches throughout the United States. If parents suspect that their children are dyslexic, they can call the toll-free number for information.

Publications include a newsletter, *Perspective on Dyslexia*, an annual journal, *Annals of Dyslexia*, and a free pamplet, "What Is Dyslexia?"

Gifted

Council for Exceptional Children (CEC), 1920 Association Drive, Reston, VA 22091 (703) 620-3660

This is the only professional organization that is dedicated to improving the quality of education for all exceptional children, both handicapped and gifted. CEC maintains the most complete collection of special-education literature in the world through its Department of Information Services and the ERIC Clearinghouse on Handicapped and Gifted Children. A number of publications are available through their catalogue.

Gifted Child Society (GCS), 190 Rock Road, Glen Rock, NJ 07452 (201) 444-6530

This parent-advocacy group provides educational enrichment and support services for gifted children and their families. Services include workshops, programs for preschoolers, clinical services, remediation for school-age children, seminars, and conferences. GCS also sponsors competitions and bestows awards.

Publications include a semiannual newsletter and advocacy packets, such as "How to Help Your Gifted Child."

National Association for Creative Children and Adults, 880 Spring Valley Drive, Cincinnati, OH 45236 (513) 631-1777

This organization provides assistance and direction to individuals and groups seeking to enlarge the scope of their creative talents. A counseling and evaluation service is available at their headquarters in Cincinnati. Other services include regional and national conferences, programs, and projects in creativity that can be conducted in the home or at school.

Publications include *The Creative Child and Adult Quarterly*, which contains insights into theories and applications of creativity research. Also available are compilations of creative writing, vignettes, musical compositions, and the *Three-Way Developmental Growth Check List for Giftedness-Talent-Creativity*.

National Association for Gifted Children, 4175 Lovell Road, Suite 140, Circle Pines, MN 55014 (612) 784-3475

This is an advocacy organization dedicated to the needs of the gifted. It promotes research and development into the nature and education of the gifted and disseminates information on gifted children to parents and others.

Publications include the *Gifted Child Quarterly* and *Communique*, a newsletter.

Books on Early Education

Ames, Louise Bates, Ph.D., and Joan Ames Chase, Ph.D. *Don't Push Your Preschooler*, rev. ed. New York: Harper & Row, 1980.

Advice on how to relax and let your preschooler develop naturally.

Anderson, Richard C., et al. (preparers). *Becoming a Nation of Readers: The Report on the Commission of Reading*. Pittsburgh, PA: The National Institute of Education, 1985.

Based on current research, the Commission recommends steps for schools and parents to take to help children become lovers of words and books.

Anderson, Winifred, Stephen Chitwood, and Deidre Hayden. *Negotiating the Special Education Maze: A Guide for Parents and Teachers*. Englewood Cliffs, NJ: Prentice Hall, 1982.

A practical, step-by-step handbook. Revised edition (1988) available in paperback from Woodbine House.

Armstrong, Thomas, Ph.D. *In Their Own Way: Discovering and Encouraging Your Child's Personal Learning Style.* Los Angeles: Jeremy P. Tarcher, 1987.

Discusses the concept of learning differences as opposed to learning disabilities and how to help children develop their own learning styles. Hardcover. Also available in paperback from St. Martin's.

Athey, Margaret, and Gwen Hotchkiss. *Complete Handbook of Music Games and Activities for Early Childhood.* West Nyack, NY: Parker/Prentice Hall, 1982.

More than 300 activities to build basic music skills, concepts, facts, and appreciation in children ages four to eight.

Auerbach, Stevanne, Ph.D. *Choosing Child Care: A Guide for Parents.* New York: E.P. Dutton, 1981.

Step-by-step advice, including a checklist to use in evaluating each type of facility and specific questions to ask of staff, plus how to interview prospective baby-sitters. Paperback.

Balaban, Nancy, Ed.D. *Learning to Say Goodbye: Starting School and Other Early Childhood Separations.* New York: New American Library, 1987.

Strategies to turn first goodbyes into good growth experiences. Practical, warm, and reassuring. Paperback.

Balter, Lawrence. *Dr. Balter's Child Sense: Understanding and Handling the Common Problems of Infancy and Early Childhood.* New York: Poseiden/Simon & Schuster, 1985.

Compassionate and wise book on child rearing by celebrated psychologist and radio counselor. Paperback.

Boegehold, Betty D. *Getting Ready to Read.* New York: Ballantine, 1984.

A practical manual that emphasizes reading aloud. Also discusses how to integrate reading-readiness activities into your daily life. Paperback.

Briggs, Dorothy C. *Your Child's Self-Esteem: The Key to Life.* New York: Doubleday/Dolphin, 1975.

How to create strong feelings of self-worth in your child is the focus of this calm, sensitive approach to child rearing. Briggs believes self-esteem gives children the strength to meet stress and the courage to become committed, responsible, productive, creative, and humane adults. Paperback.

Burtt, Kent Garland, and Karen Kalkstein. *Smart Toys: For Babies from Birth to Two.* New York: Harper/Colophon, 1981.
Seventy-seven easy-to-make toys to stimulate your baby's mind. Paperback.

Butler, Dorothy. *Babies Need Books.* New York: Atheneum, 1980.
Sound advice on the importance of books and literature to the raising of caring and competent human beings. Inspirational.

Butler, Dorothy and Marie Clay. *Reading Begins at Home: Preparing Children for Reading Before They Go to School.* Portsmouth, N.H.: Heinemann, 1982.
Practical, commonsense guidance about reading, supported by research, is presented in this clear manual, which answers parents' questions and offers sound advice. Paperback.

Caplan, Frank, and Theresa Caplan. *The Second Twelve Months of Life: Your Baby's Growth Month by Month; The Early Childhood Years: The 2- to 6-Year-Old.* New York: Bantam, 1977, 1983.
Each book is a mini-course in child development and covers physical development, language acquisition, and stages in a child's learning. Paperback.

Caplan, Frank, ed. *The First Twelve Months of Life: Your Baby's Growth Month by Month.* New York: Grosset & Dunlop, 1971.
Excellent overview, with charts. Available in hardcover and paperback.

Carr, Rachel. *Be a Frog, a Bird or a Tree: Creative Yoga Exercises for Children.* New York: Harper & Row, 1977.
Instructions, with clear photographs.

Cohen, Dorothy. *The Learning Child.* New York: Random House, 1972.
Drawing on the findings of psychologists like Piaget and her own experiences teaching child development at New York's Bank Street College, the author shows how parents can turn a child's

curiosity into a lifetime talent for learning. Hardcover. Also available in paperback (1988) from Schocken Books.

Cohen, Dorothy and Virginia Stem. *Observing and Recording the Behavior of Young Children.* New York: Teachers College Press, 1974.

Demystifies what teachers look for and find in children's behavior. Written in a warm, clear, and detailed style. Hardcover. Third revised edition (1983) available in paperback.

Cole, Ann. *Purple Cow to the Rescue.* Boston: Little, Brown, 1982.

Hundreds of imaginative activities organized in useful categories. Available in hardcover and paperback.

Dodson, Fitzhugh, Ph.D., and Ann Alexander, M.D. *Your Child: Birth to Age 6.* New York: Simon & Schuster, 1986.

Developmental milestones plus advice on how to stimulate your child's intellect, language development, and emotional growth. Paperback.

Dombro, Amy Laura, and Leah Wallech. *The Ordinary is Extraordinary: How Children Under Three Learn.* New York: Simon & Schuster, 1988.

Discusses how to make everyday chores stimulating learning occasions for your child and more satisfying for you.

Ehrlich, Virginia Z. *Gifted Children: A Guide for Parents and Teachers.* Englewood, NJ: Prentice Hall, 1982.

Answers parents' questions about gifted children from preschool through college age. Includes characteristics, parent and teacher roles, I.Q. tests and what they mean. Available in hardcover and paperback.

Einon, Dorothy. *Play with a Purpose: Learning Games for Children Six Weeks to Ten Years.* New York: Pantheon, 1985.

Suggestions for activities as well as tips on toys and books to buy. Each activity is accompanied by an explanation of its educational value and information about the child's developmental stage.

Elkind, David. *The Hurried Child: Growing Up Too Fast Too Soon.* Redding, MA: Addison-Wesley, 1981.

Ground-breaking look at the pressures on children today. Offers advice, insight, and hope for solving problems. An important book.

Elkind, David, *Miseducation: Preschoolers at Risk.* New York: Knopf, 1987.
The author warns against the dangers of early and inappropriate instruction for young children. He shows how miseducation can damage a child's future learning and discusses what parents should look for when deciding upon the initial stages of their child's education and preschool programs. Compelling and insightful. Available in hardcover and paperback.

Erikson, Erik. *Childhood and Society,* 2d ed. New York: W.W Norton, 1963.
Erikson's classic work on the social significance of childhood. The author presents his theory of life-cycle and the eight stages of development, each with its associated "crisis." Also available in paperback (1986).

Fisher, John J. *Toys to Grow With: Endless Play Ideas That Make Learning Fun.* New York: Perigee/Putnam, 1986.
By the cocreator of Johnson & Johnson Developmental Toys. Includes play tips and ideas for homemade toys. Paperback.

Forisha, Bill E., Ph.D., and Penelope B. Grenoble, Ph.D. *Creating a Good Self-Image in Your Child.* Chicago: Contemporary, 1988.
Chronological discussion of developmental stages as related to self-image and advice on how to help your child maximize his or her positive qualities. The authors emphasize the importance of feeling lovable and worthwhile. Paperback.

Gerard, Patty Carmichael, with Marian Cohn. *Teaching Your Child Basic Body Confidence.* Boston: Houghton Mifflin, 1988.
The Gerard method for enhancing physical development through creative play, for children birth to six years. Author asserts that physical self-assurance is the basis of self-confidence and self-reliance. Paperback.

Glazer, Tom. *Eye Winker, Tom Tinker, Chin Chopper: A Collection of Musical Fingerplays.* New York: Doubleday, 1978.

With musical arrangements for piano and guitar chords. Available in hardcover and paperback.

Goff, Paul E. *Nature, Children and You*, rev. ed. Athens, OH: Ohio University Press, 1981.
How adults can help make the outdoors more meaningful to children. Practical ideas for activities. Available in hardcover and paperback.

Graves, Donald, and Virginia Stuart. *Write from the Start: Tapping Your Child's Natural Writing Ability*. New York: EP Dutton, 1985.
How to encourage your child's interest in writing and reading at home and how to work with teachers to improve writing instruction in the schools. Based on Graves's seminal research in the field. Available in hardcover and paperback.

Grilli, Susan. *Preschool in the Suzuki Spirit*. San Diego: Harcourt Brace Jovanovich, 1987.
An outline of the Suzuki philosophy and method of musical instruction plus an account of the Suzuki Preschool and its students in action. This inspiring book has educational implications beyond the realm of music training. Paperback.

Gross, Beatrice and Ronald, eds. *The Great School Debate: Which Way for American Education?*. New York: Touchstone/Simon & Schuster, 1985.
Sourcebook on the controversy over quality in the schools. Available in hardcover and paperback.

Gurian, Anita, and Ruth Formanek. *The Socially Competent Child: A Parent's Guide to Social Development—From Infancy to Early Adolescence*. Boston: Houghton Mifflin, 1983.
How parents can help their children develop a concern for others while maintaining their own rights. Includes topics such as friendship, moral judgments, manners, and troubled times.

Healy, Jane M., M.D. *Your Child's Growing Mind*. New York: Doubleday, 1987.
Current scientific research on the biology of the brain and children's learning is presented clearly. Author feels parents can help

children better if they understand how children learn. Comprehensive, warm, and informal style. Refutes the "superbaby" myth.

Hearne, Betsy. *Choosing Books for Children: A Commonsense Guide.* New York: Delacorte, 1981.
Specific recommendations of age-appropriate titles, written with warmth and humor by the children's book-review editor of *Booklist.*

Holt, John. *How Children Learn.* New York: Pitman, 1967.
Author believes children have a natural style of learning, which is often warped by later training. Hardcover. Also available in paperback (1986) from Dell.

Kaye, Evelyn. *The ACT Guide to Children's Television: How to Treat TV with TLC,* rev. ed. Boston: Beacon Press, 1979.
How to maximize benefits and minimize damage from children's exposure to TV. Paperback.

Kaye, Peggy. *Games for Reading: Playful Ways to Help Your Child Read.* New York: Pantheon, 1984.
More than seventy easy-to-follow games. Available in hardcover and paperback.

Kimmel, Mary Margaret, and Elizabeth Segel. *For Reading out Loud!: A Guide to Sharing Books with Children,* rev. ed. New York: Delacorte, 1988.
Excellent introduction convincingly makes the case for reading out loud. Includes annotated and indexed recommendations for what to read and for which ages and occasions.

Kobrin, Beverly. *Eyeopeners!: How to Choose and Use Children's Books About Real People, Places and Things.* New York: Viking, 1988.
Excellent annotated and indexed list of books, with ideas for follow-up activities.

Lansky, Vicki. *Vicki Lansky's Practical Parenting Tips for the School-Age Years.* New York: Bantam, 1985.
Includes help for homework hassles. Paperback.

Leach, Penelope. *Your Baby and Child: From Birth to Age Five*. New York: Knopf, 1977.

Arranged by developmental stages, with coverage of physical and emotional growth and attention to language acquisition, play, and learning. Practical advice. Available in hardcover and paperback.

Lynch-Fraser, Diane. *Danceplay: Creative Movement for Very Young Children*. New York: Walker, 1982.

Fosters a child's social and intellectual growth through physical expression in a spirit of creative play; for children eighteen months to four years.

Marzollo, Jean, and Janice Lloyd. *Learning Through Play*. New York: Harper & Row, 1972.

Actvities are arranged according to skills they foster. Written with clarity, enthusiasm, humor, and affection. Available in hardcover and paperback.

Miller, Jo Ann, and Susan Weissman, M.S.W. *The Parents' Guide to Daycare*. New York: Bantam, 1986.

This is a comprehensive and clear guide on how to select and evaluate day-care facilities, with an emphasis on health and safety. The book also gives practical advice on how to make daycare a happy, problem-free experience for all. With tips such as how to help your child adjust to separation and how to lessen the "hurry-up-let's-go" hassles of morning. Paperback.

Osman, Betty B. *Learning Disabilities: A Family Affair*. New York: Warner, 1980.

How parents can help children overcome learning disabilities at home and at school. An appendix lists resources, diagnostic tests, tools, and legal rights. Paperback.

Pogrebin, Letty Cottin. *Growing Up Free: Raising Your Child in the 80's*. New York: McGraw-Hill, 1980.

Nonsexist approach to child rearing that seeks to nourish the unique person in every child. A warm, compassionate, commonsense book that touches all aspects of a child's life, including school and learning.

Princeton Center for Infancy; Frank Caplan, ed. *The Parenting Advisor*. New York: Anchor/Doubleday, 1978.

Research and advice on all areas of child rearing, from health and nutrition to learning and social, sensory, and emotional development of your child. Paperback.

Rioux, William, and the Staff of the National Committee for Citizens in Education. *You Can Improve Your Child's School: Practical Answers to Questions Parents Ask Most About Their Public Schools.* New York: Simon & Schuster, 1980.
Comprehensive.

Rogers, Fred, and Barry Head. *Mr. Rogers' Playbook: Insights and Activities for Parents and Children.* New York: Knopf, 1975.
TV's celebrated Mr. Rogers offers more than 335 games and projects to help children understand the world around them, foster self-expression, independence, fairness, curiosity, creativity, and character and to encourage family interaction. Hardcover. Also available in paperback (1986) from Berkley.

Rubin, Zick. *Children's Friendships.* Cambridge, MA: Harvard University Press, 1980.
How friendships develop and a child's concept of friendship changes with increasing cognitive sophistication. Covers topics such as popularity, peer pressure, cliques, fads, and conformity. Available in hardcover and paperback.

Saul, Wendy, with Alan R. Newman. *Science Fare: An Illustrated Guide and Catalog of Toys, Books and Activities for Kids.* New York: Harper & Row, 1986.
Invaluable to stimulating interest in science and nurturing intellectual curiosity. Superb bibliography of books for children. Includes section on computers. Available in hardcover and paperback.

Sears, William, M.D. *Creative Parenting: How to Use the Concept of Attachment Parenting to Raise Children Successfully from Birth to Adolescence,* rev. ed. New York: Dodd-Mead, 1987.
Covers developmental stages; also, special-needs children. Paperback.

Segal, Marilyn, Ph.D., and Don Adcock. *Your Child at Play: Birth to One Year/ One to Two Years/ Two to Three Years/ Three to Five Years.* New York: Newmarket, 1985.
A four-volume series that discusses and describes how chil-

dren learn from play and provides hundreds of detailed suggestions for activities to encourage exploration, self-confidence, coordination, social and physical development, and character. Paperback.

Sobol, Tom and Harriet. *Your Child in School: Kindergarten Through Second Grade.* New York: Arbor House, 1987.

What to expect from your child's school, how to help your child get the most out of it, and what to do if something goes wrong. Includes learning differences of many kinds. There are three other volumes in this series, covering third through fifth grade, sixth through eighth grade, and ninth through twelfth grade.

Solomon, Alan M., Ph.D., and Penelope B. Grenoble, Ph.D. *Helping Your Child Get Top Grades.* Chicago: Contemporary, 1988.

Guidelines for understanding your child's needs and talents and strategies for solving problems and maximizing academic potential. Paperback.

Stein, Sara Bonnett. *New Parents' Guide to Early Learning.* New York: New American Library, 1976.

What your child can and cannot be expected to do in the first few years and how you can help your child learn to talk, wonder, solve, and invent. Paperback.

Stock, Claudette, M.A., and Judith S. McClure, Ph.D. *The Household Curriculum: A Workbook for Teaching Your Young Child to Think.* New York: Harper/Colophon, 1983.

Imaginative and easy-to-use workbook using common household objects to stimulate children's learning. Spiralbound paperback.

Stocking, Holly S., Diana Arezzo, and Shelley Leavitt. *Helping Kids Make Friends.* Allen, TX: Argus, 1979.

Clear, warm, practical advice on how adults can help children gain confidence and social skills to make friends. Paperback.

Taylor, Denny. *Family Literacy: Young Children Learning to Read and Write.* Portsmouth, NH: Heinemann, 1983.

The author looks at families where children have sucessfully learned to read in order to extract patterns of family life that nurture literacy skills. Written in a warm, reasssuring, and informal style. Paperback.

Taylor, Denny, and Dorothy S. Strickland. *Family Storybook Reading*. Portsmouth, NH: Heinemann, 1986.
    The importance of sharing books with children and information and advice on the best ways to do so. Warm, reassuring, inspiring, and practical, with many recommended readings. Everything you need to know to get your child off to a good start in reading. Paperback.

Touw, Kathleen. *Parent Tricks-of-the-Trade*. Washington, DC: Gryphon/Acropolis, 1987.
    Includes sections on activities to promote interest in science, art, and music. Paperback.

Trelease, Jim. *The Read-Aloud Handbook*, rev. ed. New York: Viking Penguin, 1985.
    How to coax your child away from television and into books; what to read and when to begin. Paperback.

Turecki, Stanley, M.D., and Leslie Tonner. *The Difficult Child*. New York: Bantam, 1985.
    A step-by-step approach for understanding and managing hard-to-raise children. Available in hardcover and paperback.

Velez, Gail Granet. *The Parents' Resource Book*. New York: New American Library, 1986.
    Practical advice on child rearing, from infancy through toddlerhood, with sections on play, day-care and nursery schools. Paperback.

Weiss, Sol. *Helping Your Child with Math*. Englewood Cliffs, NJ: Prentice Hall, 1986.
    Strategies, activities, and games that parents can use to help their children learn and enjoy elementary-school math. Available in hardcover and paperback.

White, Burton L. *The First Three Years of Life*, rev. ed. Englewood Cliffs, NJ: Prentice Hall, 1985.
    Author describes in detail the physical, emotional, and mental development of the young child. He emphasizes the importance

of the first three years to lifelong learning. A classic. Available in hardcover and paperback.

Wiener, Harvey S. *Talk with Your Child: How to Develop Reading and Language Skills Through Conversation at Home.* New York: Viking, 1988.
    Provides an overview of language acquisition. Reassuring and practical.

Williams, Robert A., Robert E. Rockwell, and Elizabeth A. Sherwood. *Mudpies to Magnets: A Preschool Science Curriculum.* Mount Rainer, MD: Gryphon, 1987.
    Useful ideas for the home as well. Paperback.

Wolf, Aline D. *Mommy, It's a Renoir!: Art Postcards for Art Appreciation—A Parent and Teacher Handbook.* Altoona, PA: Parent Child Press, 1984.
    A manual on art appreciation for the young with activities to delight both child and adult. Paperback.

Wolpert, Sheila, and Beth Levine. *Playgroups: From 18 Months to Kindergarten—A Complete Manual for Parents.* New York: Pocket Books, 1988.
    How to set up and organize your own playgroup, help your child adjust, plus activities. Paperback.

Zaslavsky, Claudia. *Preparing Young Children for Math: A Book of Games.* New York: Schocken, 1979.
    More than 100 games and activities arranged in order of difficulty, according to the way children learn. Available in hardcover and paperback.

Zimbardo, Philip G., and Shirley L. Radl. *The Shy Child: A Parent's Guide to Preventing and Overcoming Shyness from Infancy to Adulthood.* New York: McGraw-Hill, 1981.
    Based on research conducted at Stanford University and tested by the Stanford Shyness Clinic. Hardcover. Also available in paperback (1982) from Doubleday.

Juvenile Books Relating to Early-Childhood Education

Ancona, George. *Helping Out*. New York: Clarion Books, 1985.

An exploration, in black-and-white photographs, of the pleasures and special relationships of adults and children working together. For ages 3–7.

Anno, Mitsumasa. *Anno's Math Games*. New York: Philomel Books, 1987.

Simple and complex mathematical concepts are presented as games. Observant parents will think of similar learning opportunities hiding in real-life "games." Inspirational and perfect for sharing with kindergarten-age upward.

Arnosky, Jim. *Drawing Life in Motion*. New York: Lothrop, Lee & Shepard, 1984.

A book to teach you how to see things before you try to draw them. For ages 10+.

Banks, Kate. *Alphabet Soup*. Illustrated by Peter Sis. New York: Knopf, 1988.

A grumpy boy, who doesn't want to eat his lunch, dips his spoon into his alphabet soup, pulls out a string of words, and enters into a fantastic adventure. Fun for beginning and prereaders as they enjoy identifying the noodle letters scattered over the pages. For ages 3–8.

Blue, Rose. *I Am Here: Yo Estoy Aqui*. Illustrated by Moneta Barnett. New York: Franklin Watts, 1971.

Luz, a little Puerto Rican girl, attends kindergarten for the first time. While it is difficult adjusting to a new country, a new school, and a new language, her warm relationship with her teacher helps Luz adjust and gain confidence. For ages 4–7. Out of print, but available in most libraries.

Breinburg, Petronella. *Shawn Goes to School*. Illustrated by Errol Lloyd. New York: Crowell, 1974.

A heartwarming and simple story of a young black child's first day at nursery school. This book is gently humorous and reassuring as Shawn overcomes his initial shyness and smiles a teeny-weeny smile. For ages 2–5.

Brown, Laurene Krasny and Marc. *Visiting the Art Museum*. Illustrated by Marc Brown. New York: E.P. Dutton, 1986.
   A humorous and informative introduction to museums and their treasures. An excellent way to prepare for, remember, and just talk about the visit. Tips for parents on how to make the trip enjoyable for all are appended. For ages 4–8.

Brown, Marc. *Play Rhymes*. New York: E.P. Dutton, 1987.
   These twelve cheery rhymes, complete with easy-to-follow fingerplays, will delight parent and child. Old favorites and new, to challenge the youngest.

Brown, Margaret Wise. *The Runaway Bunny*. New York: Harper & Row, 1972.
   The little bunny tries to run away from his mother, but she won't let him. Told in rhythmic, repeated prose, this classic reinforces the concept of the stability of familial security and love. For ages 1–6. Available in hardcover and paperback.

Burns, Marilyn. *I Am Not a Short Adult!: Getting Good at Being a Kid*. Boston: Little, Brown, 1977.
   Love, responsibility, television, school, and how to decide for yourself what kind of kid you want to be. For ages 9–12. Available in hardcover and paperback.

Burns, Marilyn. *The I Hate Mathematics Book!* Boston: Little, Brown, 1975.
   Events, gags, experiments, and activities to change math haters into math enthusiasts. For upper-elementary-school age.

Cobb, Vicki. *Skyscraper Going Up!* (A Pop-up Book). New York: Crowell, 1987.
   Explains about building construction in clear text, detailed pictures, and three-dimensional and moveable pop-ups. For ages 6–10.

Cohen, Miriam. *Will I Have a Friend?* Illustrated by Lillian Hoban. New York: Macmillan, 1967.
   Reassuring story of a small boy's fears of going to school and

not having any friends. Cohen has written several other books about Jim and his school friends, each title dealing sensitively and entertainingly with the school life of these ethnically diverse children. For ages 3–8. Available in hardcover and paperback.

Duvoisin, Roger. *Petunia*. New York: Knopf, 1962.
Petunia, that silly goose, thinks that if she owns a book she will be wise. Eventually, she learns that it's what's inside a book that counts, and she resolves to learn to read. For ages 4–7.

Gibbons, Gail. *Dinosaurs, Dragonflies and Diamonds: All About Natural History Museums*. New York: Four Winds, 1988.
A first look at museums, including staff, collections, exhibits, and programs. Useful for preparing children for a visit. For ages 6–8.

Gibbons, Gail. *Sun Up, Sun Down*. San Diego: Harcourt Brace Jovanovich, 1983.
Elementary scientific facts presented in vibrant, primary-colored pictures, accompanied by a brief text. For ages 4–8.

Greenfield, Eloise. *Me and Neesie*. Illustrated by Moneta Barnett. New York: Crowell, 1975.
Neesie, Jannel's best friend, wasn't real. But that was okay until Jannel started school. A sensitive look at young growing pains. For ages 4–7. Available in hardcover and paperback.

Haldane, Suzanne. *Painting Faces*. New York: E.P. Dutton, 1988.
An introduction to face painting and its significance in various cultures. Intriguing color photos make this fun for browsers, too. For ages 3+.

Hest, Amy. *The Crack-of-Dawn Walkers*. Illustrated by Amy Schwartz. New York: Macmillan, 1984.
It's Sadie's turn for an early-Sunday-morning walk with Grandpa: to the bakery, to get the paper, to enjoy a cup of cocoa together, and finally home through the snow, making the first footprints in it. For ages 4–7.

Hoban, Tana. *Shapes, Shapes, Shapes*. New York: Greenwillow, 1986.
This is a photographic tour de force of common objects, high-

lighting their geometric shapes and helping children and adults think about shapes, relationships, and "looking at things." Rich material for discussions between adult and child. For ages 3–8.

Isadora, Rachel. *Willaby*. New York: Macmillan, 1977.
While the other first-graders are busy with their lessons, Willaby is drawing. She is always drawing. A charming story about a little girl who is a little different. For ages 4–7.

Jonas, Ann. *Where Can It Be?* New York: Greenwillow, 1986.
A little girl looks all over for her missing blanket. Turn the half pages and help her search. A playfully instructive book that will engage young children in using words and in "reading" pictures. For the youngest.

Kohl, Herbert and Judith. *The View from the Oak*. New York: Macmillan (Sierra/Charles Scribner's Sons), 1977.
This fascinating and marvelous book explains how other creatures such as dogs, whales, bees, snakes, and ants experience the world. For ages 9+. Available in hardcover and paperback.

Kraus, Robert. *Leo the Late Bloomer*. Illustrated by Jose Aruego. New York: Windmill, 1971. Reprint New York: Simon & Schuster, 1987.
Reassuring and simple tale of a small tiger who couldn't read, write, or do anything right. But Leo finally blooms in "his own good time." For ages 3–7.

Macaulay, David. *Castle/Cathedral/City/Pyramid/Unbuilding*. Boston: Houghton Mifflin.
Outstanding books that explain in great detail the construction of great architecture. Inspirational and fascinating. For ages 9+.

MacDonald, Suse. *Alphabatics*. New York: Bradbury, 1986.
Letters are transformed into objects and incorporated into illustrations: "O" becomes an owl, "U" an umbrella. Bold, bright, outstanding graphics. Fun with letters leads to fun with language. For ages 4+.

Raboff, Ernest. *Art for Children* (series). Philadelphia: Lippincott.
This series presents briefly, directly, and imaginatively the

works and lives of sixteen major artists. In addition, the author guides children in how to look at a painting and inspires a better understanding of art. For ages 9+.

Rockwell, Harlow. *My First Nursery School.* New York: Greenwillow, 1976.
  Cheerful watercolors illustrate this happy introduction to leaving home for school. Rockwell captures the feelings of accomplishment and pride that young children feel about their nursery school. Of special interest are pictures of men in nurturing roles. For ages 4–7. Available in hardcover and paperback.

Rogers, Fred. *Going to Daycare.* New York: Putnam, 1985.
  Reassuring text and bright, colorful photographs explain what it is like to go to day care. Mr. Rogers tells young children that they will still have their own special place in the family and that they will meet new friends and caring adults at day care. An opportunity for parents to prepare their child for a new experience. For ages 2–5. Available in hardcover and paperback.

Schwartz, David. *How Much Is a Million?* Illustrated by Steven Kellogg. New York: Lothrop, Lee & Shepard, 1985.
  Humorous picture book helps children and adults conceptualize the immensity of large numbers. For ages 4+.

Striker, Susan. *Young at Art: The First Anti-Coloring Book for Preschoolers.* New York: Fireside/Simon & Schuster, 1985.
  A "coloring book" that inspires children to draw, color, or paint however they like, with limitless possibilities. Helpful tips for parents include song and play activities to stimulate creativity. Paperback.

Tompert, Ann. *Will You Come Back for Me?* Illustrated by Robin Kramer. Niles, IL: Albert Whitman, 1988.
  Suki's mother allays her daughter's fears by imaginatively showing her that she loves her far too much to abandon her at day care. For ages 2–6.

Weiss, Nicki. *Barney Is Big.* New York: Greenwillow, 1988.
  On the night before his first day at nursery school, Barney needs to talk about what it means to be a big boy. For ages 4–6.

Yashima, Taro. *Umbrella*. New York: Viking, 1958.

It finally rains and Momo is able to use her new umbrella and new boots. It is also the first time that she will walk home from nursery school without holding her mother's hand. For ages 3–6. Available in hardcover and paperback.

Index

......

Abandonment, 146–47
Acceptance, 5, 126
  of disabled child, 75, 80
  of limitations, 80
Accomplishment, 11, 83
Achievement, 10, 103, 151, 162
  academic, 169
  desire for, 65
  of learning-disabled child,
    166
  pressure for, 66–7
Achievement tests, 150, 152–53
Activities, 125, 145, 158–59
  early childhood, 61
  in art museum, 106–7
  indoor/outdoor, 131
  mathematics, 54–8
  music and dance, 112–15
  reading, 47–9
  scientific, 93–4
  spontaneous, 137
  to understand disabled, 77–9
Aggression, 26
Alphabet, 134, 142
Answering questions, 94–9
Anxiety, 67, 74, 143, 146–47
Appreciation, 115
  of disabled persons, 80
  of music, 109
Aptitude tests, 150
Arguing, 63–4

Arts, 101–15
  activities in, 106–7
  visual, 101–8
Asking questions, 45
Attention, 179, 181
Attitude, 135
  importance to reading, 43
  toward disabled, 75–6, 78–80
Authority, 60, 119, 139
Autonomy, 125, 126

Behavior, 3, 34, 94
Body awareness, 57, 93–4,
    112–13
Body language, 157–58
Books, 135
  juvenile, 201–6
  on early education, 189–200
Brain, 22, 28

Cause and effect, 92
Challenges, 60, 65–7, 80, 137,
    180
Change, 33–4, 159, 177–78
Character. *See* Personality
Chemistry, xxii
Child, needs of, 6
Childrearing, xix–xxi
Classroom conference, 170–73,
    175–76
Clinging child, 147

Collecting, 91
Color, 48–9, 107, 139–40
Comforting, 131
Communication, xxii, 12, 99, 123, 125
  art and, 106, 108
  books and, 135
  humor and, 84, 87
  in classroom conference, 170–73
  learning-disabled child and, 167
  newborn and, 37–8
  problems in, 41
  See also Language; Reading; Speaking; Writing
Community, sense of, 134
Comparing, 52, 55–6, 57, 93, 174
Compassion, 81
Competence, 68, 85
Competing, 61, 63–5, 137
Compromising, 63–4
Concentration, 122
Confidence, 11, 66–8, 70, 123
Consideration, 11, 69–70, 78–80
Construction, 55–6
Control, 86, 105
Cooking, xxii, 54–5, 93
Cooperation, 11, 123, 133, 169
Coordination, 127, 165
Correction, 73, 74
Correspondence, 53–5
Cortex, 22, 23–4
Counting, 55, 123
Courage, 156
Courtesy, 69, 73
  See also Consideration; Manners
Creativity, 46, 104, 106, 155, 174

Criticism, 66, 171–72, 181
Culture, 10, 119
Curiosity, 11, 90, 99, 141, 180
  about disabilities, 76–7
Curriculum, 132

Dance, 111–15
Day-care centers, 124
Development, 5, 163, 177–78
  drawing and, 102–3, 105
  of brain, 28
  of language, 37–42
  of memory and perception, 27
  of reading skills, 43–4
  of social skills, 59
  of vision, 23–4
  psychological, 22
  rate of, 33–4
Developmental appropriateness, 124–26
Dexterity, 142
Direction, 140
Disabled child, 75–6, 119, 132, 151, 164
  help for, 80–2
  integrating into mainstream, 75–84
  interaction with, 78–9
  rights of, 81
  siblings of, 82–3
Disappointment, 151, 154, 167
Discipline, 131, 167–68
Discovering, 6, 89, 94
DNA, 24–5
Down's syndrome, 77
Drawing, 46, 91
  action, 102–3
  challenges of, 101
  parent help in, 102–8
Drills, 139
Dyslexia, 119

Early childhood education, 121–35
Education
  early childhood, 121–35
  quality of, 149
Educational philosophy, 132, 172
Education for All Handicapped Children Act, 165
Egocentricity, 59, 69
Elementary school. *See* Grade school
Emotional problems, 163
Encouragement, 11, 94, 115, 126, 158, 180
  to draw, 46
  to read, 43
  without pushing, 34, 159
Enthusiasm, 7, 94, 156, 158–59
  for science, 90
  learning and, 26, 122
Environment, 122, 132, 158, 167
  academic, 137
  for play, 7–8
  for studying, 174, 176
  interpretation of, 10
  learning, 124, 160, 178
  personality and, 25
  stimulating, 24, 139
Ethnic stereotypes, 10
Expectations, 70, 153, 157, 175
  experience and, 72
  in primary school, 137–39
  of disabled children, 81
Experience, 6, 22, 56, 90, 179–80
  away from home, 138
  enrichment by, 34
  expectations and, 72
  familiar, 96

for gifted child, 161
math concepts and, 52, 54
personality and, 25, 156
physical growth and, 23–4
social, 67–8
Experimentation, 4, 27, 92, 133, 139
  art and, 104–5, 108
  with skills, 34
Experiments, 93–4
Explaining, 96–7
Exploration, 94, 99
  in music, 109
  of bodies and movement, 112–14

Failure, 27, 65, 66
Fairness, 63–4
Fear
  of disabilities, 76–7, 83
  starting-school, 143–48
Feedback, 70
Feelings, 171–72, 181
  manners and, 69–70, 74
  of disabled children, 81
Field trips, 134
Flexibility, 26, 156, 162
Friends, 8–10
  with disabilities, 79–80
  See also Playmates
Frustration, 63, 64–5, 168
  drawing and, 104
  of disabled children, 81
  of gifted children, 160

Games, 60–2
  in art museum, 106–7
  parental role in, 63–4
  shy child and, 68
  to understand disabilities, 79
Gardening, 94

Genetic code, 24–5
Gifted children, 152, 155–62
Grade school
  first-day fear, 143–48
  getting ready for, 137–54
Grouping, 52–3, 92
Guilt, xx–xxi, 82

Head Start, 122
Heredity, 25, 164
Homework, 173–76
Humor, 162
  bathroom, 85
  different types of, 87–8
  encouragement of, 87–8
  health and, 84
  importance of, 84–8
  parental help and, 87–8

Image, 65
Imagination, 8, 49, 123, 141,
  156, 174
Imitation, 40
Independence, 123, 126, 142
  173
Individual Education Plan, 166
Individuality, 11, 127, 157–58
Infants. *See* Newborns
Inhibition, 26
Initiative, 174
Instruments, 109, 111
Intelligence quotient, 149–51,
  155
Interfering, 64
Intervention, 5, 42
Introverted child, 67
Inventiveness, 11, 40, 101–4

Jokes, 86

Key episodes, 130–31
Kindergarten, 121, 123, 132–33

Labeling, 68, 80, 152
Language, 37–49, 125, 127,
  141, 167, 180–81
  descriptive, 90–1
  development of, 37–42, 165
  humor and, 84–5
  parents and, 41–2
  patterns of, 40
  quirks in, 42, 95
  testing of, 152
  understanding of by infant,
  28
  See also Communication;
    Reading; Speaking;
    Writing
Laughing, 87
Learning, 12
  early experiences, 5
  hands-on, 133
  incidental, 10–11
  natural love of, 4, 7, 29, 35
  nervous system and, 22
  parental involvement in, 7
  personality and, 26–7
  play and, 5–12, 129, 133–34
  self-esteem and, 26–7
  self-initiated, 6–7
  tactics for, 27–9
  value of, 119
Learning disabilities, 163–68
Library, 47, 78
Limitations, 167
Listening, 45, 96, 122, 140, 157
  in classroom conference, 172
  to children, 98–9
Loyalty, 123

Manners, 69–75
Matching, 53–4, 56–7, 139
Mathematics, 51–8
  parental help and, 54–8
  testing of, 152

Maturity, 137, 142
  emotional, 9, 138, 151
  rate of, 33
Mealtime, 72, 131
Measuring, 55, 57, 134
Memorization, 139
Memory, 27
Mind-body relationship, 21–9
Mislabeling, 85
Mistakes, 47, 65, 181–82
Money, 57
Montessori Program, 126–27
Motivation, 12, 151, 163, 169
  internal, 66
  manners and, 70
Motor coordination, 101
Motor skills, 104
Movement, 111–15, 125, 127
Music, 109–15
  activities in, 113–15
  formal lessons in, 110–11
  listening to, 109–10

National Association for the
  Education of Young
  Children, 124–25, 130, 132
Neatness, 11, 138
Negotiation, 9, 123
Nervous system, 21–2
Newborns, 27
Numerical relationships, 139
Nursery school, 121, 123–24,
  128
Nurturance, 9, 94, 158
Nutrition, 11, 163, 179

Objectivity, 171–72
Observation, 4, 63, 89, 90, 157
Open classroom, 128
Opportunities, 159, 178–79,
  181
Optimism, 11, 151

Pantomime, 91
Parent-child relationship, xxi, 5
Parents
  art experience and, 103–8
  as role models, 10–1
  humor and, 87–8
  language development and,
    41–2
  participation in reading, 43–
    6
  roles of, xix, 3–4, 177
  scientific thinking and, 89–90
Parent-teacher relationship,
  169–73
Part/whole relationships, 54,
  56
Patterns, 48, 51, 53
Perception, 27
Performing, 115
Persistence, 167
Personality, 25–7, 156, 157
Pessimism, 27
Phonics, 46
Play, 4, 6, 60–4, 125
  as learning, xxiii, 5–12, 133–
    34
  drawing and, 104–5
  for disabled children, 81
  setting for, 7–8
  with pets, 93
Play groups, 129
Playmates, 8–10
  for gifted child, 161
  language development and,
    40–1
  social skills and, 68
  with disabilities, 79–80
  See also Friends
Playthings. See Toys
Point of view
  of child, xx, 74
  of others, 59

Position, 140
Positive reinforcement, 11
Praise, 11, 68, 167, 181
Prereading practice, 48–9, 141–42
Preschoolers, 9, 179
  gifted, 160–62
  language development of, 39–40
  movement and dance, 111–12
Preschool, 121–22
  choice of, 129–35
  curriculum of, 124
  developmentally appropriate, 124
  selection of, 123–26
  types of, 126–29
Pressure, 66–7, 105
Prewriting skills, 141–42
Pride, 9, 11, 46, 134, 148
Problem solving, 64–5, 101–2, 104, 125
Public problems, 71–2
Punishment, 11, 76
Puzzles, 57

Questions, children's, 94–9

Reading
  aloud, 44, 141, 145
  early learning of, 28–9
  fun of, 43–8
  preparation for, 43–9, 127
  See also Communication; Language
Resentment, 162
  of siblings, 82, 148
Resources
  books on early education, 189–200
  for disabled children, 81–2, 186–88

for gifted child, 161, 188–89
  juvenile books, 201–6
  organizations, 183–89
Respect, 35, 106, 126, 133, 139, 170, 181
  manners and, 69
  of disabled persons, 78–80
Responsibility, 173–74, 176
Restating, 42
Rewards, 66
Rhythm, 111–15
Riddles, 86
Risk-taking, 27, 81
Role models, 73, 158–59
Rote exercises, 139
Routine, 168
Rules, 9, 60, 72, 143
  concept of, 62–3
  explanation of, 73
  for homework, 174–76
  inconsistency of, 40–1
  manners and, 69–70

Schools. See Grade school; Kindergarten, Nursery school; Preschool
Science, 89–99
Security, 123, 144–47
Self-centeredness, 59, 69
Self-control, 74
Self-discipline, 174
Self-esteem, 11–2, 65, 71, 126, 131, 151, 157, 159, 162, 163, 168
  formal music lessons and, 111
  learning and, 26–7
  manners and, 70
  of disabled children, 80–1
  shy child and, 68
Self-expression, 46, 81
Self-image, 12, 27, 162

891

Senses, 27, 90, 124, 127
Sentence structure, 46
Separation, 143–44, 146, 148
Sequencing, 53, 56–7
Setting table, 55
Sex roles, 10
Shapes, 48, 51, 107, 139,
   142
Sharing, 9, 54, 123, 138
Shyness, 67–9, 70
Siblings, 148
   of disabled children, 82–3
Similarities and differences,
   91, 93–4, 139, 150
Singing, 110
Sizes, 51, 139
Skills, 8, 81, 126
   at games, 63
   athletic, 156
   computational, 52
   coping, 7–8
   early learning of, 3
   language, 7–8
   motor, 140–41
   practical, 138–39
   problem-solving, 64, 125
   "school readiness," 137–
   54
   science, 90–2
   sequencing, 45
   small-motor, 125
   testing of, 150
   See also Social skills
Social interaction, 9
Social skills, xxi-xxii, 9, 59–88,
   133, 138, 140, 166
   and disabled child, 82–3
   at mealtime, 131
   humor and, 88
   importance of play in, 60–4
   shyness and, 67–9
Sorting, 52–3, 56–7, 91–2

Speaking, 12, 22, 28, 41
   parental correction of, 41–2
   See also Communication;
      Language
Special-needs children, 77–8,
   82
      See also Learning
      disabilities
Standardized testing, 148–54
Storytelling, 46
Strategies
   changing, 66
   in drawing, 103
   problem-solving, 64–5
Stress, 126, 131, 164, 179
   humor and, 88
   of change, 33–4
   of disabled children, 81
Study habits, 174
Success, 65, 102, 125, 152
   in school, 169–76
Suggestions, 105
Support, 126, 158–59, 180–
   81
   of shy child, 68
Symbols, communicating
   with, 49

Teacher-pupil ratio, 131–32,
   137
Teacher's role, 3–4, 127, 128,
   145
Television, 10
Telling, 96–7
Testing
   I.Q., 149–51
   learning-disabled children,
      165–66
   multiple-choice, 153
   standardized, 148–54
Thinking, 51, 98
Time, 53, 55, 140

Timetable, 163
  natural, 22, 23
  rushing of, 33
Toddlers, 9
  development of vision in,
    23
  movement and dance
    among, 111
Toys
  age-appropriate, 7–8,
    139
  educational, 160
  structured/unstructured, 8
  uses for, 34
Transition times, 130–31, 143–
    44
Trial and error, 27–8, 126
Trust, 123, 170
Turn-taking, 133, 138

Uniqueness, 24–5, 94
  of child's gifts, 157–58
  of disabled child, 80, 83

Value
  of drawing, 105
  of reading, 47
Values, 157
Violence, 10
Vision, 23–4, 28, 141
Visual arts, 101–8
Vocabulary, 37, 150, 180
  mathematics and, 58

Walking, 22
Winning, 60, 61–3
Word endings, 39–40
Word meaning, 38–9, 47
Word order, 39
Word play, 86
Words, taboo, 86
Work, xxiii
Writing, 28, 91
  getting ready for, 43–9, 127
  with child, 46
  See also Communication;
    Language